CONTENTS

The Rolex Awards
for Enterprise

PREFACE

TREE Of LIFE: Buddhism And Protection Of Nature, was published in 1987 expressly to be recycled; not — heaven forbid! — turned into pulp, but the full contents or any of its parts to be used, and reused, by anyone or any group anywhere finding the information helpful; not requiring formal permission but only requesting proper attribution, and a copy of use for our archives. As an element in Buddhist Perception of Nature's educational outreach, the book was provided as a gift while copies lasted in response to every request from environmental protection groups, religious scholars, scientists, students, schools, universities and libraries in more than 30 countries.

The scope of interest internationally held many surprises. One of the first published translations of the full text was in Hungarian. Among the first environmental protection conferences inviting ***TREE Of LIFE*** as a major educational component was called "Ecology and Religion", organised in fact on the Buddhist Perception of Nature "blueprint", and took place in Mexico City. College-level courses on ecology in several universities in Europe and America were employing ***TREE Of LIFE*** as a textbook within a year of its publication. Requests for copies poured in from Buddhists, Catholics, and even communist cadres in Vietnam.

It soon became clear that the little book was in its own ironic way an illustration of a problem of conservation. Limited supplies dwindled at the same time human demand increased. Many conservationist colleagues were recycling the materials in just the way originally envisioned. The Buddhist Publication Society in Sri Lanka republished the entire English text in their BUDDHIST PERSPECTIVES ON THE ECOCRISIS, for example. But many around the world who did not have a copy of the original source wanted one. Flawed human planning, which is freely admitted here, is another illustration of success — or failure — for conservation of resources in the face of the unexpected.

Buddhist Perception of Nature project personnel anticipated interest, but not to the extent that came about, and so quickly. It was believed many conservationists around the world felt that a focus on spirituality and humanitarian values highlighted in religions was urgently needed in the work, but the number of people and sense of urgency had been underestimated. There was confidence the first comprehensive teaching tool ***TREE Of LIFE*** would help fill a void, inspire further work and contribute to a growing school of environmental ethics, but Buddhist Perception of Nature had been designed as a project, a catalyst for other projects, not as an institution. The ultimate response to the book was not imagined, and there was no provision for a second printing.

Only now are we able to publish again. As anyone involved with non-profit organisations knows, this kind of work, needed as it may be, cannot be carried out without support from people and groups in a position to help, who are both generous and concerned — in this project, with cultural integrity, ethics, environmental protection, and the health of future generations of all life on earth.

The 1999 edition of ***TREE Of LIFE*** is the reprint called for, and more — it updates and expands educational materials and sources of information. This new volume is once again provided to researchers, educators, students, schools and libraries.

The ACKNOWLEDGMENTS recognise contributors to Buddhist Perception of Nature's work in many different forms, and to publication of this book in both editions. But special mention must be made of Mr. and Mrs. Hans Michael Jebsen, Dean Steven C. Rockefeller, The Sacharuna Foundation and The Alliance of Religions and Conservation in making this new edition possible.

A decade has passed since the first edition, invoking more irony; Buddhist Perception of Nature specifically called for a sense of urgency in environmental protection. A decade, however, has a certain time framework of substance that His Holiness the Dalai Lama invoked in a Message for Wildlife Conservation International/New York Zoological Society's "Conservation for the Twenty-first Century":

> ***"The beginning of the twenty-first century is only a few years away, and such a landmark in time provides a good focus for life's values and directions. A year, a century, or a millennium ends, another begins. For much life on earth, however, cycles are coming to an end, not just because of natural selection, but as a result of human destruction, born out of ignorance, greed, and lack of respect for other forms of life."***

The past recent years have witnessed many messages urging protection of nature based on both science and ethics from His Holiness the Dalai Lama, whose leadership in this field has been cited in The Nobel Peace Prize in 1989 and the United Nations Environmental Programme's Earth Prize in Environmental Ethics in 1991 among many other international awards.

A growing number of other spiritual leaders have spoken out to heighten awareness and action for nature protection, and in all this forward looking progress we've been taken back to the roots of environmental ethics, which have always been with us but too often set aside in pursuit of short-term material goals.

Although we didn't know it at the time our project got underway, the first group to focus international ecumenical attention on Saint Francis of Assisi in contemporary forms of environmental education had just started up in Europe. Prof. J. Ronald Engel, whose outstanding dedication to environmental ethics matched by management skills, had resulted in making him a one-man international clearing house of information, put Buddhist Perception of Nature in touch with Dr. Marisa Cohen, founder of Assisi Nature Council, based on the same thesis, with the same shoestring budget and established for Roman Catholics, and all Christians, and all others for that matter, at the same time, in the same spirit our Buddhist work was launched.

Ron Engel also had information on more than 50 other, similar groups established in the mid 1980s. Late as it all may have been in arising, clearly something special was happening — spontaneously, involving many different faiths in many parts of the world. Some attribute this remarkable widespread flourishing of attention to environmental ethics to inspiration. But creative approaches to problems, like trees and all plants, wildlife, and humans, too, grow with strength only in healthy ecosystems. In this case, again with irony, with the growing evidence of the planet's ill health, arose a tide of concern about uncontrolled pollution and vanishing species — the general, growing and alarming evidence of destruction of the Earth — that began in the 1960's.

Rachel Carson's *SILENT SPRING* in 1962 was published as a special interest little book that became a wake-up call of amazing proportions. New York Zoological Society sent George Schaller to Africa, and when his *THE YEAR Of THE GORILLA* appeared in 1964 it was another milestone; here was a scientific work that became a popular book in the best-seller market, and it centered on the fate of an endangered species that is a very near relative of mankind. IUCN (International Union for Conservation of Nature and Natural Resources) and WWF (originally World Wildlife Fund, now World Wide Fund for Nature), both designed to operate internationally, were established at that time, along with hundreds of groups working at national levels in dozens of countries.

The conservation movement continued to grow, and some of the most impressive offshoots established the world's first ever "green" political parties in the early 1980's. But in recent times, interest, awareness and action for protection of nature has been phenomenal in all realms.

In 1986, the World Wide Fund for Nature (WWF) International, building upon work begun earlier by the Buddhist Perception of Nature, the Assisi Nature Council and other similar work in different faiths, called the first ever interfaith meeting of major religions on the theme of ecology. Held at Assisi, it brought together Buddhism, Christianity, Judaism, Hinduism and Islam. At the meeting each faith issued a core statement of its teachings on religion and ecology and committed itself to work on practical projects.

Tens of thousands of new groups at community, municipal, provincial, regional, state and international levels were established around the world. Governments, even if only largely in lip service, and multi-national corporations even if only largely for marketing and future profits' purposes, have recognised the importance of protection of nature and natural resources. The EARTH SUMMIT convened by the United Nations in 1992 in Brazil, and many other conferences and meetings in many parts of the world have brought together governments, non-governmental and grassroots organisations, and private industry in a common cause, in a spirit of cooperation never known before.

By 1995, WWF had again brought together representatives of faiths at Windsor Castle, and the number of faiths committed to statements and action had grown to nine — the Baha's, Sikhs, Jains and Taoists had joined. In the same year it was known that more than a hundred thousand religious based conservation projects had been launched, often with initial help from WWF. The UN recognised this in the award they gave to Prince Philip in that year saying that WWF's religions and conservation network had reached "untold millions with the conservation message who could not have been contacted by any other means."

From reforesting scared forests in India, through conserving Taoist sacred mountains in China to multi-faith environmental education in Zambia to regeneration of monastic lands in Russia, religion and conservation worked together. To celebrate this and to further this work, WWF and two other funds, MOA Japan and Pilkington Trust UK, launched the Alliance Of Religions And Conservation (ARC) — the largest international programme in this field of work — which now co-ordinates the work of nine faiths and more than 15 conservation groups who collaborate to further protection of the environment, and has identified more than 120,000 religious environmental projects around the world. Such growth, from 50 only 15 years ago, is profoundly inspiring and encouraging for everyone involved.

This second edition has been long awaited, but we feel, timely now as never before, on the brink of the 21st Century and poised to help in its own small way, all the positive changes that must come about for the health of the planet and survival of life on earth as we know it.

Respecting the highly regarded contributions by the late Sir Peter Scott, and Dr. Chatsumarn Kabilsingh and Dr. Nay Htun in the first edition, we have made no changes to their texts. This is a decision that also supports the wishes of people long associated with the book and the requests of those who will only have copies in the second edition. Chatsumarn and Nay Htun, both experts in their fields and Buddhists, continue to devote work to a better, more peaceful, and protected world of rich natural and cultural diversity.

The first edition's Introduction by the late Sir Peter Scott remains as the best we could ever welcome, and our tribute to an exceptional man who generously provided so much help to Buddhist Perception of Nature and countless other conservation groups and efforts.

Thousands of entries now exist in bibliographies highlighting protection of nature, science, religious teachings, and the environmental ethics literature and projects that bring the subjects together. Books have been joined by an impressive list of films, events, broadcasts, and websites. A small book such as ours, which includes two languages of what we feel are basic, essential Buddhist Perception of Nature texts, cannot even begin to list them, although it is essential to note that such a vast treasurehouse of information, knowledge and philosophical exploration is growing, and with the growth of modern technology, more than ever within reach.

Appendices are a straightforward but important addition. Appendix I lists international organisations we have most depended on for information about the state of the global natural environment, plus those groups Buddhist Perception of Nature has worked with most closely on environmental ethics. Appendix II presents some of the most relevant messages in our project's work.

No two people are in complete agreement about what must be included in limited space. Of what has been left out, there is a wealth of philosophy, poetry and important inspiration that could fill a great many much larger books than ***TREE Of LIFE*** . Published here is a generally agreed synthesis — after much soul searching, and a bit of editorial board arm wrestling — of some of the bedrock teachings we describe as universal, and we hope will continue to inspire all who read this book.

ACKNOWLEDGMENTS

Buddhist Perception of Nature was inspired by the wisdom, and compassion and prayers for all sentient beings, of His Holiness the XIV Dalai Lama of Tibet. As an internationally respected spiritual leader, embodiment of the Tibetan Buddhist Bodhisattva of Compassion, expressed often in his own words 'a simple monk', and among a great number of other duties, Patron of Buddhist Perception of Nature, His Holiness has been tireless in taking the message of human responsibility and compassion for all life on earth, now and for future generations, to the growing world of conservation awareness.

Individuals and groups representing many different faiths, cultural traditions and disciplines from around the world have provided support in many different ways for Buddhist Perception of Nature's goals and achievements, and we recognise them here to express our sincere thanks for their interest and help.

Very special gratitude goes to Hans Michael and Désireé Jebsen, whose outstanding and enduring support for Buddhist Perception of Nature and education about environmental ethics everywhere have made both the 1987 volume of ***TREE Of LIFE*** and this 1999 edition possible.

INSTITUTIONS:

Alliance of Religions and Conservation (ARC)
American Buddhist Congress
Appropriate Technology for Tibetans (ApTT Trust, UK)
Au Sable Institute
Beldon Fund
Buddhism and Nature Protection in Thailand (BNPT)
Buddhist Library/Research Society Singapore
Buddhist Peace Fellowship
Buddhist Publication Society, Sri Lanka
Buddhists Concerned for Animals
California Community Foundation
Center of Analysis of Environmental Change
Centre for the Study of Buddhism and Peace
China Research and Exploration Society (CERS)
Clean Up The World
Council on the Sustainable Development of Central Asia (CoDoCa)
Council for Religious and Cultural Affairs of His Holiness The Dalai Lama
C S Fund
Dhammanaat Foundation for Conservation
Department of Information and International Relations, Tibetan Government-In- Exile
Earthcare (Hong Kong)
Earth Ethics Research Group, USA
ECO-ED, Canada
Foundation for Universal Responsibility of His Holiness The Dalai Lama
Friends of the Earth (Hong Kong)
Heron Fund
Future Generations Network (Foundation for International Studies, U. of Malta)
Humane Society of the U.S. (HSUS)
ICOREC
Humanitas
Indian Society of Naturalists (INSONA)
International Campaign for Tibet
International Crane Foundation
International Institute for Buddhist Studies, Japan
International Institute for Environment and Development (IIED)
International Network of Environmental Scientists (INES)
International Network for Religion and Animals (INRA)
L. J. Skaggs and Mary C. Skaggs Foundation
Monitor International
Munro Foundation
New World's Eve Foundation
Rolex Awards for Enterprise
Sacharuna Foundation
"Spirit and Nature" Conference (Middlebury College, Vermont)
The Assisi Nature Council
The Mandate for Life on Earth
The William Holden Wildlife Foundation
The Tibet Fund
The Scherman Foundation
The Snow Leopard Trust
Universidad Autonoma Metropolitana, Mexico City
Wild Camel Protection Foundation
Wildlife Conservation International, New York Zoological Society (NYZS)
William and Charlotte Parks Foundation
World Wide Fund for Nature Hong Kong
World Wide Fund for Nature Thailand
World Wildlife Fund U.S.
United Nations Environment Programme (UNEP)

INDIVIDUALS:

Ven. Amchok Rinpoche
John Ackerly
Dr. Paul Aird
Karl and Kathy Amman
Cleveland Amory
Dr. Solly Angel
Sir David Attenborough
Dr. Ernesto Barba
Robbie Barnett
Dr. Gerald O. Barney
David Bell
Rev. Fr. Thomas Berry
Bhuchung Tsering
George Bortnyk
Esmond and Chryssee Bradley-Martin
Prof. Michael Buckley
Bruce Bunting
Robert H. Burns
Susan Inoue Burns
Victoria Burrows
John Calderazzo
Dr. Tyrone McNally Cashman
Dr. Leonardo Chapella
Dr. Maria Luisa Cohen
Fleur Cowles
William Conway
Richard J. Croft, Jr.
Shann Davies
Eustace D'Sousa
Ven. B. Dhammaratana
John Dolfin
Hugh and Marney Dunn
Ollie Dwiggins
Prof. O. P. Dwivedi
Dr. Sylvia Earle
Prof. O. A. El-Kholy
Prof. J. Ronald Engel
Lord David Ennals
Harrison and Melissa Ford
Barbara Fowler
Michael Fox
Ven. Gelek Rinpoche
Richard Gere
Dr. Juan Grau
Pema Gyalpo
Kasur Lodi Gyaltsen Gyari
Maria Luisa Haley
Meg Hart-Hui
Rev. Fr. Rudi Heredia, SJ
Dr. Eric Hol
Irene Hsu
Dr. Nay Htun
John Isom
Dr. Chatsumarn Kabilsingh
Dale and Patricia Keller
Prof. Mohammed Kassas
Prof. Stephen Kellert
Rinchen Khando
Jill Kluge
Sharon Kwok
Dr. Boonsong Lekagul
Mickey Lemle
Lars-Eric Lindblad
Nandani Lynton
Hugh Locke
John Loudon
Elizabeth MacCormack
Dr. Brad Marden
Dario Mariotti
Tony Martorano
Dr. Al-Hafiz Basheer Ahmed Masri
Jeffrey McNeely
Rajiv Mehrotra
Kenneth S. Moss
John and Margaret Nash
Ngari Rinpoche
Humphrey and Mavis Oei
Rev. Fr. John Padberg, SJ
Pisit na Patalung
Stanley Pong
Stefanie Powers
Sanjiv Prakash
Jane Perkins
Friar Bernard Przewozny
Andrew Quinn
R.R.
Harry Rolnick
Dr. Peter H. Raven
Tom Regan
Lewis Regenstein
Johan Reinhard
Laurance R. Rockefeller
Andrew Ross
Dean Steven C. Rockefeller
Howard and Yvette Mimieux Ruby
Lynn and Irene Saunders
Thubten Samphel
Klaus Sandell
Ven. Sanghasena
Dr. Piet Schenkelaars
Sir Peter and Lady Scott
Dr. George B. Schaller
Dr. Nola Kate Seymoar
Linda Siddall
George Sinclair and Sonja Stevenson
Nigel Sitwell
Khunying Nunie Smansnid
Henry Steiner
Peter and Gillian Sutch
Dr. Brian Swimme
Dr. Lee M. Talbot
Larry Tchou
Tenzin Atisha
Tendzin Lodoe
Tenzin N. Tethong
Prof. Robert Thurman
Sander Tideman
Brian Tisdall
Dr. Mostafa Tolba
Lhasang Tsering
Craig Van Note
Dr. Michael van Walt van Praag
Mechai Viravaidya
Sven Wahlberg
Martha Walsh
Tashi Wangdi
Sirajit Waramontri
Wolfgang and Ursula Wolte
Wong How Man
Wu Tai-chow
Dr. Akira Yumya
Ven. Karma Gelek Yutok
Magnus Bartlett
Li Suk Woon
Au Yeung Chui Kwai

ORGANISATIONS:

Air India
Cathay Pacific Airways
Delta Airlines
DHL International
Earl & Associates
Glass Radcliffe & Wee
Graphic Communication Limited
Hongkong Hilton
Hyatt Regency New Delhi
The Mandarin Oriental Hong Kong
The Mayfair Hotel, New York
The Regent of Bangkok
United Airlines

INTRODUCTION

By Sir Peter Scott

This book and the project which brought it about — Buddhist Perception of Nature — are important new educational approaches to the ecological disasters resulting from man's destruction of nature, and what can be done to conserve the world's living resources.

It may seem surprising that a new educational perspective employs teachings and traditions, some of which date back more than 2,500 years. As an international movement of significance, conservation of nature, spearheaded by governments and private groups, is at most a few decades old, and is still in the process of being generally accepted. So why, in this most modern of causes, with immediate problems to be solved, would we apply our thoughts to ancient teachings?

The simple answer is that although conservation efforts increase they are outmatched by the continuing destruction of the environment. Our current attempts to solve the problem are not enough to do the job. Conservation work, for the most part, has been mounted in response to crisis, focusing on biological problems and proposing technological solutions with varying degrees of success. Yet the unsolved and ongoing, even accelerating, destruction of nature and natural resources has clearly not yet been tackled effectively on a global scale.

One reason for this is conservation's newness on the scene — although many of us now know how tragically late it has come for so many animal and plant species and their habitats. Another reason is the movement's limited manpower and resources.

Most of the world's human population have yet to realise that conservation of nature is an essential element of human progress, in economics, development, sustainable yields of food, in short the very life-support systems of our planet.

The message is valid, and vital for the well being of people now and for future generations, but it is widely ignored. Often its emphasis overlooks the various cultural, social and perceptual factors in the problem and in the potential solutions. Enlightened government and business leaders may be persuaded to become active in protection of nature because of the work's importance for future economic, or scientific purposes, but it is unlikely they will act solely for those reasons. People who protect, or destroy, do so for many different reasons. As His Holiness the Dalai Lama reminds us in his declaration, plain human greed is a major cause of destruction of the natural world. This and lack of respect for other people and other living forms is often the result of an impoverished cultural environment.

Among those who actively protect, we find conservationists who never go near the wilderness, but feel a responsibility to help save it for those who do. We find pragmatic business people who want to protect their investments. Children around the world often bluntly, charmingly state that they want to protect animals because they love them.

There are scientists, leaders in their fields, who support conservation for one reason: to maintain the world's biological diversity. But I know wildlife biologists and other scientists, among them the most gifted professionals at work, who were drawn to conservation because of its aesthetic appeal. Many deep philosophical elements are involved, and education stands out as the most important long-term ingredient for successful conservation.

Buddhist Perception of Nature and its products such as this volume, are of great importance to the world conservation community, not only for Buddhist communities, but also for wherever the health of our planet is threatened.

Here we have conservation education in all senses of the phrase, beginning in the home, and reaching into formal instruction and leadership levels. Conservation is set in a cultural matrix, with emphasis on accepted traditions and codes of conduct.

The impressive scholarship in the contributions from Dr. Chatsumarn Kabilsingh, in her summary of the Buddhist role in protection of the natural world, and of Dr. Nay Htun, in his outline of the state of the environment, serve to underscore the book's message: conservation as a way of life increases the quality of life, and the Buddhist precepts of harmony and care are being increasingly reflected in modern environmental management policies.

It has been my pleasure to follow the Buddhist Perception of Nature project since its beginning, before it had a title. In 1979, the project originator, Nancy Nash, working as a consultant for the World Wildlife Fund, proposed that conservation should enlist the help of the world's religions. She also proposed that WWF should make contact with China, and then personally established the contact. It kept her busy for a number of years and earned her the title "Miss Panda". Next, Nancy was asked to help set up WWF's organisation in Hong Kong.

Her "religion to help conservation" project only got underway in 1985, but already has helped collate some of the most important Buddhist teachings regarding man's responsibilities to nature, and has increased public awareness of environmental ethics wherever it has become known.

The ethical basis of conservation has always been of fundamental importance to me in my life and work, so it is very gratifying to see this so strongly represented in the project's goals and in this book. His Holiness The Dalai Lama, Buddhist but much more — an internationally respected spiritual leader — has provided inspiration, encouragement and support for the work throughout the project's development, and we can only hope that other religious leaders will follow the example of his Declaration on Environmental Ethics published in this book, so appropriately called ***TREE Of LIFE*** .

Sir Peter Scott, CBE, DSC, FRS, (1909 – 1989), who wrote his introduction to the first edition of **TREE Of LIFE** *in 1987, was a pioneer of international conservation. He was involved with the founding and following work of IUCN and WWF. Among his many honours and distinctions, he was awarded in 1953 the CBE for establishing the Wildfowl Trust, Slimbridge, UK (now the Wildfowl & Wetlands Trust), and in 1987, the Companion of Honour bestowed by H.M. The Queen, and Fellow of the Royal Society. He was trained in biology and art, and was a professional painter, author, broadcaster and lecturer.*

AN ETHICAL APPROACH TO ENVIRONMENTAL PROTECTION

From His Holiness the XIVth Dalai Lama of Tibet

Peace and the survival of life on earth as we know it are threatened by human activities which lack a commitment to humanitarian values.

Destruction of nature and natural resources results from ignorance, greed, and lack of respect for the earth's living things.

This lack of respect extends even to earth's human descendants, the future generations who will inherit a vastly degraded planet if world peace does not become a reality, and destruction of the natural environment continues at the present rate.

Our ancestors viewed the earth as rich and bountiful, which it is. Many people in the past also saw nature as inexhaustibly sustainable, which we now know is the case only if we care for it.

It is not difficult to forgive destruction in the past which resulted from ignorance. Today however, we have access to more information, and it is essential that we re-examine ethically what we have inherited, what we are responsible for, and what we will pass on to coming generations.

Clearly this is a pivotal generation. Global Communication is possible, yet confrontations more often than meaningful dialogues for peace take place.

Our marvels of science and technology are matched if not outweighed by many current tragedies, including human starvation in some parts of the world, and extinction of other life forms.

Exploration of outer space takes place at the same time as the earth's own oceans, seas, and fresh water areas grow increasingly polluted, and their life forms arestill largely unknown or misunderstood.

Many of the earth's habitats, animals, plants, insects, and even micro-organisms that we know as rare may not be known at all by future generations. We have the capability, and the responsibility. We must act before it is too late.

This message, dated 5 June 1986, in recognition of the United Nations Environment Programme's World Environment Day and that year's theme, Peace and The Environment, was first published in Tibetan, Thai and English in the first edition of **TREE Of LIFE**. *It has since been translated into more than a dozen other languages and widely republished in scientific, philosophical and educational works around the world.*

How Buddhism Can Help Protect Nature

By Dr. Chatsumarn Kabilsingh

WAT PHAI LOM is a Buddhist temple not far from Bangkok which welcomes thousands of visitors from afar every year. The visitors are birds, open-billed storks. When residing at Wat Phai Lom during autumn and winter months, their droppings white-wash trees and temple buildings.

The monks do not mind, and bird-lovers celebrate the sight. Open-billed storks would be extinct in Thailand but for the fact their last remaining breeding ground is within the sanctuary of this temple.

Ecologists point out it is scientifically important to save this species of bird, whose sole diet is a local, rice-devouring species of snail. Without the storks, the snails would proliferate, then pesticides would be brought in, and an unnecessary, poisonous cycle would go into effect.

Buddhist precepts of personal and social conduct can take much of the credit for saving the open-billed stork in Thailand, a country which has suffered tremendous destruction of the natural environment in recent decades.

Forests, for example, covered 80 percent of the land 50 years ago; today forestland has been reduced to just over 20 percent. Many bird, animal, and plant species are in danger of extinction, and some have already disappeared.

The most tragic consequences of degraded and disappearing nature and natural resources are seen in various human rural communities where survival is a struggle.

Changing ecological conditions have resulted in frequent flooding in Bangkok; it's an inconvenience. But in parts of the country's northeast, a degraded natural environment means that annual rains do not arrive on schedule, crops fail, and many people experience a borderline existence.

While so much has been destroyed, it is worth observing that even more could have been lost, and more quickly, given the modern world's eagerness for exploitation and little regard for the consequences.

It is likely that, like the open-billed stork, much of what still survives of the natural world here is linked, in varying degrees, to the influence of Buddhism, the philosophy's focus on awareness, attitudes, and actions which should never harm, and ideally should actively help all life on earth.

This is not to say that careless, even greedy individuals involved in destruction do not consider themselves Buddhists. Just as codes of conduct regarding protection of nature vary from religion to religion, interpretations of those codes vary from person to person.

In all belief systems, human nature is diverse. In Buddhism, among the world's estimated ½ billion faithful, individuals range from the highly enlightened and pious to those who don't know what else to call themselves — a group which can be described as "Buddhists by birth certificate".

Buddhism also encourages individual perceptions, even questions and challenges on the part of each practitioner, because enlightenment is a personal path. Comparative religious studies find this an unusual feature in a major religion which also has established instutional structures.

Embodied in Buddhism, however, is much ecologists and other conservation experts explain is urgently needed if destruction of the natural environment is to be halted, and life on earth as we know it is to continue.

Teachings emphasise the importance of coexisting with nature, rather than conquering it. Devout Buddhists admire a conserving lifestyle, rather than one which is profligate.

The very core of Buddhism evolves around compassion, encouraging a better respect for and tolerance of every human being and living thing sharing the planet.

Wherever Buddhism is influential, studies will usually show some direct benefit for the natural world. In Sri Lanka, predominantly Buddhist, crowded by western standards, wildlife has not been virtually eliminated, as it has been in many parts of the world. The reason, according to researchers, is the country's largely religious and devout population.

Formal protection generally results from government action, but such actions, it is felt, would never have made much effect if they were not readily accepted by the people. Successful conservation there is based on deep philosophical convictions.(1)

Many of our *Buddhist Perception of Nature* project's Tibetan research colleagues can point to the time, in living memory, when herds of wild blue sheep, yak, deer and flocks of migrating birds would travel with Tibetan nomads, or land in the midst of human settlements — apparently sensing they were safe. For the most part they were safe from harm, because the country was Buddhist.

The situation since the Chinese takeover has tragically changed, and Tibet is now described as "ecologically devastated" in many respects. In a special report for the U N Commission on Human Rights, it is noted that large areas are now deforested, and "a once flourishing wildlife seems to have been virtually wiped out..."(2)

Buddhism's benefits to nature protection throughout the faith's history might be described as effective, in a largely passive role. Recently and increasingly, however, influential Buddhists are speaking out on the subject and helping bring about recognition of the active, even dynamic role the philosophy could play in conservation.

"Today more than ever before," His Holiness The Dalai Lama told a reporter, "life must be characterised by a sense of Universal Responsibility, not only nation to nation and human to human, but also human to other forms of life."(3)

Social critic and author Sulak Sivaraksa, described as "a Thai Buddhist voice on Asia and a World of Change", believes that however complex the world has become, the message of Buddhism is relevant, indeed even more relevant than earlier, and an important catalyst of social unity and progress.(4)

Concerned about destruction of the natural environment, and convinced Buddhism, in an active role, can bring about improved protection, Khun Sulak has added to his writings on the subject a special slide show and taped message illustrating proper Buddhist awareness, attitudes, and actions concerning Nature.

"Whether they are conscious of it or not," the narrative goes, "there is a kind of Buddhist revolt against the deterioration of Nature. It is a small revolt, because it has not yet affected the overall statistics."

"But still, this peaceful commitment means something, and if it is taken seriously, it can help bring about a strong conservationist movement in our country."

His Excellency Yasuhiro Nakasone, Prime Minister of Japan, included in his address at the Commemorative Anniversary of the United Nations in 1985, an eloquent and moving call for all nations, religions, and peoples to join together to ensure that the beauty and diversity of earth will continue.

Again we find Buddhism brought into the message, one which also urges "a new global ethic" so that the Twentieth Century may be known "as the era when coexistence and mutual respect were achieved among all peoples for the first time, and when men found a proper balance with Nature."(5)

Ancient as Buddhist lessons are, their value in modern life and contemporary needs is increasingly recognised. One reason for this, according to Thai scholar Piyadassi, is that "The Buddha emphasises the practical aspect of His teaching, the application of knowledge to life, looking into life and not merely at it."(6)

British author H. G. Wells found the subject worthy of study, and summarised, "The fundamental teaching of Gauthama (The Buddha)...is clear and in closest harmony with modern ideas. It is beyond dispute the achievement of one of the most penetrating intelligences the world has ever known."(7)

Buddhism, moreover, brings a special dimension to any studies or projects such as the *Buddhist Perception of Nature*, involving education. It is the duty of every practising Buddhist to seek to replace ignorance with knowledge and wisdom. Teachers are respected; in the case of the faith's greatest teachers, revered.

To provide teachers with the tools they need to lead their students to conservation practises, project scholars have the task of thoroughly researching the vast and rich Buddhist literature, involving several languages, and early texts reaching back in some cases more than 2,500 years.

Research is the first stage, followed by assembly of the materials. For the first time, Buddhist teachings about humankind's needs and responsibilities concerning animals and plants, forests and water resources, indeed the whole natural environment, are being compiled by the *Buddhist Perception of Nature* project to produce comprehensive, educational instruments.

The wealth of material scholars are discovering is not surprising when one considers Buddhism's focus on compassion, the forest-dwelling and meditation in natural surroundings important to many in the *Sangha* — the order of monks — and the rich symbolism associated with many species of animals and plants.

Monks, for example, are forbidden to cut down trees, and know well the story of a monk long ago, who cut a tree's main branch. The spirit of the tree complained to Buddha, that by doing so, the monk had cut off his child's arm.(8)

Another teaching relates that travellers, after having rested in the shade of a large banyan, on leaving began to cut down the tree. Their actions were condemned. The tree had given them shade, much like a friend, and to harm a friend is indeed an act of evil.(9)

Anguttara Nikaya provides a similar episode:

> *"Long ago, Brahman Dhamika, Rajah Koranya, had a king banyan called Steadfast, and the shade of its widespread branches was cool and lovely.*
>
> *Its shelter broadened to twelve leagues. None guarded its fruit, and none hurt another for its fruit.*
>
> *Now then came a man who ate his fill of fruit, broke down a branch, and went his way.*
>
> *Thought the spirit dwelling in that tree: How amazing, how astonishing it is, that a man should be so evil as to break off a branch of the tree, after eating his fill. Suppose the tree were to bear no more fruit.*
>
> *And the tree bore no more fruit."*(10)

Such teachings remind Buddhists — monks and lay people alike — of the importance of showing respect for trees which provide food, shade and protection not only for people, but for all forest-dwellers.

The results of lack of respect for trees are clearly evident today. When large areas of forest are destroyed, erosion often follows, degrading watersheds, and ultimately making farming fruitless. Animal and plant species, losing their habitats, often disappear.

Although Buddhism took root in the soil of humanity more than 2,500 years ago, at a time when people generally lived closer to nature than many do today, the consequences of improper attitudes and actions regarding the earth were known, and described in the story of a Brahmin who asked The Buddha about the cause of human decrease. This is how The Buddha answered:

> *"Since folk are ablaze with unlawful lusts, overwhelmed by depraved longings, depressed by wrong doctrines, on such as these the*

sky rains down not steadily. It is hard to get a meal. The crops are bad, afflicted with mildew and grown to mere stubs. Accordingly, many come to their end."(11)

Ideally, because of the important precept that it is wrong to take life, or even cause to take life, devout Buddhists try to live on a diet of fruit, vegetables and grains. Even in this strict observance however, awareness, mindfulness, comes in.

In consuming fruits and grains, strict practitioners should be careful not to destroy the growth of such foods. Fruit from which seed has been removed, for example, is allowable.(12)

The Buddhist rules regarding consumption of foods are lengthy and complicated, and are being examined in project activities. The most important point to remember in an introduction, such as this text, is that all human activity should be with a sense of respect and reverence for all life, with a feeling of conservation and not exploitation.

For Buddhism, all animals are within the field of human perception, with an opportunity someday to gain enlightenment. Higher beings though humans may be, Buddhism teaches that man is a part of entire nature, disregarding or abusing natural laws or trying to conquer nature at his own peril.

Buddhist Perception of Nature's chief Tibetan scholar, Ven. Karma Gelek Yuthok, provides to the subject some lovely, even tender, stanzas from the *Mahayana* traditions about compassion for living things:

"Since the doctrine of Buddha specifies compassion, those who take refuge in it should forsake harming the sentient beings with a compassionate heart."(13)

Further explaining the importance of abandoning harm to living things, Tsongkhapa(14) taught:

"The abandonment of harm to sentient beings is, to foresake all thoughts and deeds as — beating men or beasts, binding with ropes, trapping and imprisonment, piercing the noses, overburdening with loads beyond their strength, and similar activities."(15)

Similarly, Dzogchen Patul Jigme Wangpo, in his text called *The Oral Transmission of Samandrabhadra,* relates:

"As it has been said that having taken refuge in The Doctrine, one should abandon harm to the living beings, the acts that are harmful to the other beings should not be done even in ones dreams... persevere with strong efforts to protect oneself from such acts."

Not doing harm is a stage reaching to higher Buddhist attitudes towards all living things — loving kindness, compassion and altruism. On the attitude of loving kindness, The Buddha has said:

"Making, all the time, a rich and extensive offering with all that can be found in the billions of worlds to the supreme noble beings,

this merit cannot match one moment of loving kindness."[16]

Another well known and much loved teaching which exemplifies the central core of compassion in Buddhism is:

> *"Thus, as a mother with her own life guards the life of her own child, let all embracing thoughts for all that lives be thine."*[17]

Two and a half millennia ago The Buddha taught disciples that the material world — earth and universe — included the worlds of "formations", "beings", and "space". That much in such ancient teachings is apparently found by many modern physicists to be compatible with the newest advances in their field of study, is less important to Buddhists than the continuing, even growing, need for human attitudes of loving kindness in our modern world.

Centuries before contamination of the earth's water would be the widespread threat to health and life that it is today, The Buddha set down rules forbidding pollution of water resources.[18] Even detailed descriptions of how a toilet should be built were provided, specifically to protect a healthy environment.[19]

Buddhism flourished early in settings of abundant Nature, and many teachings use examples and similes from Nature to convey important messages:

> *"Suppose a pool of water, turbid, stirred up and muddied, exists. Just so a turbid mind is. Suppose a pool of water, pure, tranquil and unstirred, where a man sees oysters and shells, pebbles and gravels, and schools of fish. Just so is an untroubled mind."*[20]

As for human souls in stages of growth and enlightenment, the lotus, sacred to both Hindus and Buddhists, is the symbol:

> *"...in a pond of blue lotus, or in a pond of red and white lotus, a few blue, red, or white lotus are born in water, grown in water, altogether immersed. A few blue, red and white lotus are born in water, grow there, and reach the surface — standing up, rising, undefiled."*[21]

Many of the earth's most famous animals appear in The Buddha's teachings — tiger, elephant, and lion for example. Compassion and loving kindness are expressed for all, and in a certain place The Buddha was said to have compared his own behaviour with that of a lion's —

> *"He roars with the idea, let me not cause the destruction of tiny creatures wandering astray"*

— and even claimed the word "lion" was a term for The Buddha.[22]

Among the beautiful expressions in Buddhist literature showing mutual relation and interdependence of humankind and wildlife, there was early on a realisation that survival of certain species was in danger, and that losing such creatures diminishes the earth.

Scholars with the Pali Text Society, London, provide this particularly lovely translation of a stanza from the *Khuddakapàtha*:

"Come back, O Tigers!, to the woods again, and let it not be leveled with the plain. For without you, the axe will lay it low. You, without it, forever homeless go."

Buddhism has always celebrated the richness and diversity of the earth, and the lotus is only one among the many plant species of great symbolic importance.

All Buddhist literature records that The Buddha was born in the forest, in a grove of Sal, lovely straight backed trees with large leaves. According to legend, as soon as he was born he could walk, and in the wake of his first seven steps lotuses sprang up. Meditation as a youth was in the shade of the "Jambo", one of the myrtle of which there are around 650 species.

The Buddha's further study was in the company of the Banyan, and enlightenment and Buddhahood were achieved under the spreading branches of a tree recognised for its special, symbolic place in human faith even in its scientific name, (*Ficus religiousa*). Also known as the Bo, Boddhi or Peepul, this tree is sacred in both Buddhism and Hinduism.

With all of these species we find an example of the faith's role in protection. Because of the important symbolic value they have in the life of Buddha, they are respected, and no devout follower would deliberately harm them.

It has been interesting to learn in our researches that there seems to be a twofold way of expressing and describing nature and the natural environment in the texts — a straightforward description, and then in many cases, an analogy.

Both are drawn from what was known of life and natural surroundings of the time, and largely in the northern areas of Jambudipa, or India, and yet demonstrate an extraordinary intellectual grasp of the interdependence of life altogether, at all times.

Early Buddhists were also, clearly, deeply appreciative of Nature's beauty and diversity. In the *Sutta-Nipata*, one of the earliest texts known, The Buddha says:

"Know ye the grasses and the trees...Then know ye the worms, and the moths, and the different sort of ants...Know ye also the four-footed animals small and great...the serpents...the fish which range in the water...the birds that are borne along on wings and move through the air....."

We have abbreviated above a long passage in which, for each kind of creature, The Buddha taught,

"(Know ye) the marks that constitute species are theirs, and their species are manifold..."(23)

The *Jakata*, the richly narrated Birth Stories of Buddhism, have inspired some of the world's most beautiful art, and are abundant with poetic appreciations of the beauty of Nature. In the edition edited by Professor E. B. Cowell for the Pali Text Society in 1957, passage after passage of volumes IV and V celebrate forests and waters, and the earth's wild creatures.

Here we find an area of the earth called "Garden of Delight", where grass is ever green, in forests grow all trees whose fruit is good to eat, the streams are sweet and clean — "blue as beryl" — with shoals of disporting fish. Nearby is:

> *"...a region overrun and beautified with all manner of trees and flowering shrubs and creepers, resounding with the cries of swans, ducks and geese..."*

Next is reported the fame of an area, "yielding from its soil all manner of herbs, overspread with many a tangle of flowers," and listing a rich variety of wild animals — antelope and elephant, gaur, buffalo, deer, yak, lion, and rhinoceros, then tiger, panther, bear, hyena, otter, hare and more.

If such scenes seem "other worldly" it is because, through ignorance, greed, and lack of respect for the earth, the world's growing human population has already transformed many of the earth's gardens of delight into poisoned fields, sterile, incapable of sustaining Nature's rich diversity.

That so much of the earth has already been destroyed, and destruction is actually increasing, is insupportable for Buddhists or people of any persuasion or belief who seek knowledge and wisdom, and who feel a sense of responsibility for the condition of life on this planet now and for future generations.

In *Buddhist Perception of Nature* research we are discovering and compiling teachings which in many ways also provide shocking reminders of how much we have lost of the natural world, and in such a brief space of time. This is one of the many lessons being learned, and it adds to a feeling of urgency to complete our research, and place good educational materials into the hands of teachers who will use them well.

By doing our part to bring to light the ancient Buddhist teachings which are as valid today as they have always been, in widening circles Buddhism can be an active element in proper conservation of the natural environment.

By sharing the fruits of our work with others, we look forward to a world acceptance of an environmental ethic that will replace ignorance with knowledge, greed with generosity, and lack of respect for the earth with attitudes of compassion and loving kindness — for all life.

Dr. Chatsumarn Kabilsingh, chief Thai scholar for the Buddhist Perception of Nature Project, teaches Religion and Philosophy as a member of the Faculty of Liberal Arts, at Thammasat University, Bangkok. She is also the author of a number of popular and scholarly articles on Buddhism, the translator of the Lotus Sutra, and the Tao Te-Ching into Thai, and the author of the book, Study of Buddhist Nuns: Monastic Rules.

Footnotes:

1. Moyle, P and Senanayke, F R in FAO's TIGERPAPER, October 1980
2. TIBET: THE FACTS, by the Scientific Buddhist Association (London) 1984
3. FAR EASTERN ECONOMIC REVIEW, 3 August 1979, p. 23
4. Sulak Sivaraksa, SIAMESE RESURGENCE, published by the Asian Cultural Forum on Development (Bangkok) 1985
5. See page 16
6. Piyadassi, BUDDHISM A LIVING MESSAGE (Bangkok)
7. Nigosian, S A, WORLD RELIGIONS, published by Edward Arnold (London) 1975

8. Pacittiya, Bhutagama Vagga, THAI TRIPITAKA, Vol 2, page 347
9. *Ibid*, Vol 27, p 370
10. Anguttara Nikaya, GRADUAL SAYINGS, Vol 3, p 262
11. *Ibid*, Vol 1, p 142
12. THAI TRIPITAKA, VII, p 8
13. Tsongkhapa, GREAT EXPOSITIONS ON THE GRADUAL PATH
14. The great teacher and revitalizer of Buddhism in Tibet, 14th century A D
15. *Ibid*
16. SAMADHIRAJA SUTRA, Vol 11, Dege Version
17. KHUNDDAKAPATHA (London) by the Pali Text Society, 1960
18. GRADUAL SAYINGS, Vol 26:104, p 174
19. *Ibid*, Vol 7, p 48 *Vinaya Pataka*
20. *Op. cit.*, Vol 1, pp 6-7
21. Nissagiya 15, SACRED BOOKS OF THE BUDDHISTS (SBB), Mahavagga, XIV, p 9
22. Woodward, F L (Tr) *Ibid*, Vol V, pp 23-24
23. Fausboll, V (tr), published by Motilal Banarsidass (Delhi) 1968.

From the Address by Japanese Prime Minister, H.E. Yasuhiro Nakasone, at the Commemorative Session of the 40th Anniversary of the United Nations, 23 October 1985:

"Our generation is recklessly destroying the natural environment which has evolved over the course of millions of years and is essential for our survival.

Our soil, water, air, flora and fauna are being subjected to the most barbaric attack since the earth was created. This folly can only be called suicidal.

If we are to preserve our irreplacable Earth and ensure the survival of mankind, I believe we must create a new global ethic and devise systems to support it.

Let us act today so that future historians can look back on the closing years of the Twentieth Century as the era when co-existence and mutual respect were achieved among all peoples for the first time and when men found a proper balance with nature.

We Japanese derive our beliefs and philosophy from traditions handed down by our ancestors over thousands of years, and from later influences of Confucianism and Buddhism. Basic to our philosophy is the concept that man is born by grace of the great universe.

We Japanese generally believe that the great natural universe is our home, and that all living things should co-exist in harmony with the natural universe. We believe that all living things — humans, animals, trees, grasses — are essentially brothers and sisters.

I doubt that this philosophy is unique to the Japanese. I believe that better understanding of it could contribute much to the creation of universal values for our international community.

The human potential for creativity is distributed evenly among all peoples in all lands, and all the different religious beliefs and artistic traditions in the world are equally unique and equally valuable.

The starting point for world peace is, I believe, a recognition of this diversity of human culture and a humble attitude of mutual appreciation and respect.

Are we not destroying our environment on an unprecedented scale, and perhaps endangering the survival of all life on this planet? As a political leader, I cannot but feel a deep sense of responsibility for the situation I am witnessing.

Thus I ask you to join me in a vow. Let us vow to work together so that, in the middle of the next century, when Halley's Comet completes another orbit and once again sweeps by our planet, our children and grandchildren will be able to look up at it and report that the Earth is one, and that mankind everywhere is co-existing in harmony and working for the well-being of all life on this verdant globe."

DR. NAY HTUN, expert on the global natural environment and a humanitarian, was involved with Buddhist Perception of Nature starting in the conceptual stages and continuing generously with wise advice at every step of development. His chapter in the first edition of **TREE Of LIFE** *appeared just over a decade ago, but is considered so concise and important, well organised and written, and so splendidly embracing ethics in the conclusions, a wide range of opinion urged a reprint — exactly as the original, for the historical record.*

This we have done. Numbers and statistics have changed, but only by degrees that change constantly, but unfortunately, consistently providing evidence of increasing destruction of our waters, soils, forests, species and genetic diversity, and atmosphere.

As our second edition went to press, two new reports painted a bleak picture. Cornell University scientists announced that 40 percent of (human) deaths worldwide are caused by pollution and other environmental factors, and that climatic changes will make matters worse; global warming will bring about an increase in diseases and promote the emergence of new illnesses. The report also predicts millions of people will become "environmental refugees", forced to abandon their home areas in a desperate search for food. This is not a new situation, but emerging on a much greater scale of magnitude.

A third of the world's natural resources have been consumed in the period 1970 – 1995, according to a report published by WWF in October, 1998. The Living Planet Report seeks to present a "quantitative picture of the state of the world's natural environment and the human pressures on it."

WWF's LPI (Living Planet Index) measures change in the health of the earth's natural ecosystems since 1970, focusing on forest, freshwater, and marine biomes as these contain most of the world's biodiversity. Results showed forest cover falling by 0.5 per cent a year, making a total loss of 10 per cent between 1970 and 1995 — an area of forest disappearing every year, the size of England and Wales. Half the earth's forests have disappeared since the last Ice Age, 6,000 to 8,000 years ago, with the worst-affected region being Asia, where about 70 per cent of original forest is gone.

Freshwater ecosystems were disappearing at the rate of 6 per cent a year, and were halved in the same 25 year period of study. Marine ecosystems were also declining by 4 per cent a year, and in total dropped by 30 per cent in the same period.

Such figures according to the report's author Jonathan Loh, "are a stark indication of the deteriorating health of natural systems," He added that most concerning of all, "is the decline of freshwater lakes, rivers and wetlands — among the most productive and diverse environments in the world..."

Data on threatened species, consumption of grain, fish, wood, cement, fresh water, forest cover, marine species and carbon dioxide emissions from 152 countries compiled the LPI, adding to important information from many sources about decline of the quality of life today, and picturing an even more degraded planet tomorrow.

By the time any reader absorbs this text, tomorrow is now. Nay Htun's message is more relevant than ever, and the richness of earth's biodiversity, quality of air and water, and progress of civilisation depends on decisions made and actions taken urgently and without fail. The earth itself may survive without human life, but human life cannot survive with an utterly destroyed earth.

THE STATE OF THE ENVIRONMENT TODAY:

THE NEEDS FOR TOMORROW

By Nay Htun

DURING THE PAST 30 YEARS the world has witnessed unprecedented growth. As a result vast amounts of natural resources have been and continue to be consumed, and in the process critical life-support systems and the state of the environment are being affected. There is growing concern that these changes could have serious and irreversible consequences for planet earth.

The scale of change can be measured with a few stark statistics: every year 20 million hectares of arable land is lost; 12 million hectares of tropical forests are destroyed; 25 billion tonnes of top soil are washed away; and 3,000 billion tonnes of soil and rock are moved in mining operations.

At the same time, water consumption has increased from 3,000 cubic kilometres in 1980 to 3,750 in 1985. Commercial fuel consumption is now the equivalent of 7,500 million metric tonnes of oil, almost double the amount 20 years ago, and the number of motor vehicles has increased from 50 million in 1950 to 410 million in the early '80s. Most significantly, the population is now growing by more than a billion every 15 years, so that by the end of the century it will be six billion — double the number of people in 1960.

These awesome figures tend to numb the mind, but it is quite clear that planet earth has been subjected to tremendous misuse and abuse. It has been stripped, leveled, filled, extracted, dried, flooded and denuded of vegetation on a scale that stretches to the limit the earth's power to assimilate.

In this article I will offer a brief overview of the state of the air, water, soil and forests; describe some of the many technical, economic and institutional measures being undertaken to correct the degradation and reverse the trend; and finally suggest some of the measures that need to be taken to promote development activities that will improve not only standards of living but also the quality of life, by using resources rationally, and with minimal impact on the environment — in short sustainable development.

In conclusion I want to advocate strongly the imperative need to embody the ethical dimension of compassion, tolerance, respect for all forms of life, and responsible stewardship of the earth.

The state of the environment

An increasing amount of information and data on the environment is now available. In 1982 the United Nations Environment Programme, UNEP, undertook a detailed and comprehensive review of the state of the environment. UNEP also publishes annually State of the Environment Reports that focus on different topical issues. Similarly, Brown (1986) produces yearly State of the World reports. And recently the World Resources Institute (1986) provided an assessment of the resource base that supports the entire world's economy. In addition, at the national level an increasing number of countries issue state of the environment reports.

The atmosphere

There are a number of air quality crises confronting the world. These are 'acid rain' precipitation, the increase of 'greenhouse gases' and destruction of the ozone layer.

'Acid rain' is the phenomenon where sulphur and nitrogen oxides, released from the combustion of fossil fuels and natural sources such as volcanic eruptions are scavenged by clouds and cause rain and snow to become acidic. About 180 million tonnes of these oxides are emitted every year, and carried over distances of 1,000 km and more.

The death of lake fish in Scandinavia and North America has been directly attributed to the leaching of toxic metals from the soil. While there is as yet no unanimous agreement that acid rain is the cause of this or the large scale destruction of forests in Europe, there is growing acceptance that it is one of the main causes, either directly or indirectly by triggering other weakening mechanisms. Acid precipitation is also responsible for accelerated deteriorations of priceless buildings, monuments and statues. The rusting of ferrous metals and the need to repaint are often, thereby, increasing the economic costs as well as the cultural.

Turning to the build-up of 'greenhouse gases', there is now compelling evidence that increased concentrations of gases such as carbon dioxide, carbon monoxide, methane, nitrous oxides and chloroflurocarbons, which control the earth's ozone layer could lead to a climatic warming through the greenhouse effect. In terms of quantity, carbon dioxide build-up is by far the largest. Between 1950 and 1980 it increased at an average rate of four percent a year.

Basically, the presence of greenhouse gases produces an insulating effect. They permit higher energy solar radiation to reach the earth's surface. In turn the earth radiates low energy rays. Some are lost in outer space but some are absorbed by the greenhouse gases, which warm up the atmosphere.

This warming process has been understood since the 1930s and has been a matter of much earlier speculation. During the past decade more research has been undertaken and at the UNEP/WMO/ICSU Conference on Greenhouse Gases, Climatic Change and Associated Impacts held in 1985 in Villach, Austria, the international consensus was that if atmospheric carbon dioxide concentrations were to double, the global mean temperature would increase by 1.5 to 4.5 degrees Centigrade. Wind, ocean current and precipitation patterns would change, causing sea levels to rise between 20 and 140 cm., and many coastal cities will be under water. There will also be profound effects on global ecosystems, agriculture and water resources causing immense social and economic consequences.

Just as crucial is the damage being done to the ozone layer, which occurs high in the stratosphere. Ozone absorbs short wave-length ultra-violet radiation, letting only the far less harmful longer wave-length rays reach the earth. However, when the ozone concentration is depleted or the layer destroyed, more UV rays pass through the stratosphere.

The major substances which deplete the ozone layer are two nitrogen oxides, water molecules and chloroflurocarbons commonly used as aerosel can propellants and refrigerants. The response of human skin to sunlight is most pronounced at the higher wave-lengths, and the most common effect is sunburn, but two types of skin cancer can result, one of them often fatal.

An increase in the amount of ultra-violet rays reaching the earth's surface will also affect vegetation. The U.S. National Crop Loss Assessment Network reported that at a concentration of 0.12 parts per million of ozone, a peanut crop was 50 percent smaller than a similar crop grown under ideal conditions. Changes in stratospheric ozone would also affect heating rates, air movements, penetration of infra-red radiation and water vapour concentrations.

Water and its uses

The total volume of water is about 1,400 million km^3 and changes very little. However, more than 97 percent of the total is sea water. Only 0.01 percent is "fresh" and readily available. The remainder is locked in the polar ice caps, in depths of more than 75 meters, or in the atmosphere as water vapour. This relatively meagre quantity of available water is often wasted.

Accurate data for water withdrawals are not available, but rough estimates on total water use was about 3,000 km^3 in 1985. Irrigation accounted for 73 percent, followed by industry's 21 percent and 6 percent for domestic use.

The gross area under irrigation worldwide increased from about 28 million to 50 million hectares between 1960 and 1985. Despite this intensive use, irrigation is only 30-50 percent effective. Excessive use of ground water in relatively dry areas has depleted aquifers and improper design and management of irrigation systems have caused salinization, alkalination and waterlogging.

Industrial uses of water in developed countries have been decreasing in the last decade because of increased efficiency and recycling. In the U.S., Japan and

West Germany, for example, water is used in the plant at least twice before it is discharged. However in developing countries industrial water consumption rates have been increasing with industrial growth and there is an urgent need for conservation measures.

Public uses of water, for drinking, sanitation and sewage, although making up a small percent of the total, have very important effects on human health. Three out of five people in developing countries do not have easy access to safe drinking water and nearly 2 billion people are exposed to diseases by drinking contaminated water. As regards sanitation, three out of four people in the developing world do not have any kind of sanitation system.

Water pollution is a well-known problem. The inland waters of many countries are experiencing over-enrichment by nutrients from agricultural fertilizers and domestic sewage, causing heavy growths of algae. The widespread increase of nitrogenous fertilizers in many rivers and ground waters is also causing concern. Untreated sewage degrades the quality of the water and in most developing countries the coliform content is so high that it is unfit for human consumption.

With increasing industrialization, the quantity and variety of pollutants discharged have also increased. Although impressive efforts have been made and technical progress achieved in the treatment of industrial water pollution, there is growing concern about non-biodegradable toxic chemical pollutants that are in trace quantities, making them difficult to detect with conventional instruments and hard to remove from the water.

The productivity of the marine environment and its capacity to disperse pollutants depend on its physical and chemical properties, which are affected by sewage, agricultural chemicals, oil and metals. It has been estimated that about 25 billion tonnes of materials are added to the ocean each year, over 90 percent via rivers.

Coastal zone developments affect extensive areas of mangroves and coral reefs. Mangroves play an important part in the economics of tropical countries, and for millenia they have constituted a crucial habitat for many unique plants and animals. Mangrove ecosystems also support commercial fishing and provide living space for more than 2,000 species of fish, invertebrates and plants. Yet, globally less than 1 percent of the world's mangroves are officially protected.

Coral reefs are possibly the most productive ecosystems in the world. Although they occupy only 0.1 percent of the earth surface, about 10 percent of the world's fish catch is associated with the reefs. Also, coastal communities in the tropics derive much of their subsistence needs, security and cultural utility from coral reefs, which are now facing degradation from pesticides.

The state of the soil

The world at present has about 1.5 billion hectares of arable land under cultivation. It is estimated that each year about 25 billion tonnes of valuable top soil are lost. About 6 billion hectares, or 40 percent of the earth's land surface are desert, and every year from 5-7 million hectares of arable land become desert. The major causes are heavy grazing during droughts and overstocking, or population pressures which result in extreme subdivision and fragmentation of land holdings.

For irrigated lands the main desertification problems are waterlogging and salinization, which affect all regions of the world. Meanwhile forests and woodlands are lost through over-logging for fuel and timber, clearing for agriculture, fires and overgrazing. Since the affected areas are commonly watersheds, deforestation leads to increased run-off and flooding, accelerated water erosion and siltation, which often extend into adjacent lower-lying areas of land use.

By the year 2000, the WRI (1986) study reported, there would be about 0.5 hectare of cropland per person in the industrialized world, about 0.25 hectare in centrally planned economics and an average of 0.19 hectare in the developing countries. That means areas with the greatest need tend to have the least available land.

Among the types of soil degradation included in the process of desertification, erosion is one of the most widespread. Depending on local conditions, soil loss and new soil formation are approximately in balance at an erosion rate of 0.5 to 2 tonnes per hectare per year. Agriculture, especially on steep slopes, increases the rate substantially. Lost soil may be carried away by wind and water. One reason erosion is difficult to control is that many of its costly impacts occur miles away from the eroding field. Off-site effects of erosion include damage to fish and coral reefs, loss of hydropower potential, lower storage capacity in reservoirs, and increased need for dredging rivers and harbours. In the U.S. the off-site costs of erosion are estimated to be US$16 billion.

The rapid rise in the population is the immediate cause of deteriorating food-production systems. Growing populations have a fixed supply of arable land, but too often diminish its quality and quantity. As the demand for food increases, agriculture is extended onto marginal land and traditional techniques for keeping erosion in check and land productive, such as terracing, crop rotation and fallowing, are breaking down.

One indication of the rate of erosion is the size of the sedimentation loads of the Yangtse, Ganges, Amazon, Mississippi and Mekong rivers, which now total 3,883 million tonnes a year.

The death of forests and species

Tropical forests provide mankind with a wide range of benefits. They supply over half of the raw ingredients needed by the pharmaceutical industry; essential oils, latex, fibers, dyes, resins and gums; and protective watersheds that regulate water flows to more than a billion farmers downstream. Furthermore tropical forests are home to some 200 million people who rely on them for their fuel, food, shelter and animal fodder; and diverse species, 20 to 30 times greater than in temperate forests. According to the WRI (1986) report, about 1.7 million species have been indentified. A widely accepted minimum is 5 million and many scientists believe that the total could exceed 10 million. At least 75 percent of these species are estimated to occur in tropical zones.

The extinction of species has occured since the dawn of time, but the rate has accelerated alarmingly recently. Some have predicted that by the end of the century a further million species could be lost. A major reason is the destruction of habitats, particularly tropical forests. Deforestation is due to slash and burn farming, logging, cattle ranching, construction of hydroelectric dams, human settlements and highway construction. While there has been increased efforts recently to reforestation schemes, the rate of deforestation is five to 10 times greater. Also reforestation is primarily focused on single-species plantations, which have far less diversity than natural forests, often with non-indigenous trees for commercial use. It is estimated that annually about 12 million hectares of tropical forests are lost.

How can we improve the state of the environment?

The measures that have been undertaken are numerous and far ranging, using institutional, technical and economic approaches.

While in 1972 there were about a dozen countries with Ministries or Departments of the Environment, now almost all have some form of institutional means of managing the environment. In addition most countries have strengthened and revised environmental legislation and many have promulgated new ones to deal with emerging problems such as acid rain, toxic chemicals and hazardous wastes.

At the regional level an increasing number of organisations have been formed to enhance environmental cooperation. In Asia and the Pacific these include the ASEAN Expert Group on the Environment, the South Asia Cooperative Environment Programme, and the South Pacific Regional Environment Programme. The OECD's Environment Committee has a very active programme to foster cooperation among member states and, recently, the African Ministers for Environment met and launched the Cairo Plan of Action. Similar efforts have also been made in Latin America and the Caribbean. The need for regional cooperation is underscored by the 11 programmes of the UNEP Regional Seas Programme with participation of 120 countries.

At the international level, there are now more than 80 multilateral treaties available to protect the environment and wildlife and encourage the rational use of natural resources. These include the Convention on International Trade of Endangered Species and the 1980 World Conservation Strategy prepared by the International Union of Conservation of Nature and Natural Resources (IUCN) with the cooperation and financial assistance of UNEP and WWF and the collaboration of FAO and UNESCO.

Recognising the importance of environmental education, many if not most schools now include the subject in their curricula. An expanding array of teaching aids is being developed and used to promote environmental education. At the tertiary level the number of institutions offering courses on the environment has also increased appreciably. In Asia and the Pacific, for example, there are at least 248 institutions with courses related to the environment, and more are offering post-graduate courses.

The media has also played a significant role in increasing environmental awareness. Almost all newspapers regularly carry articles on the subject, and environmental accidents, such as Sveso, Bhopal, Chernobyl and the Rhine received extensive coverage.

This increase in awareness has prompted people to become interested in and concerned with environmental matters. One of the most significant developments in the past two decades has been the growing involvement of the public in protecting nature. Individuals and groups have formed associations to do something positive. These include the Chipko Movement to stop deforestation and the People's Forestry Movement of India to enlist the cooperation of villagers and plant a million trees and the 100 Million Trees Programme of Sri Lanka.

Technical measures available to treat gaseous, liquid and solid wastes are many, and technology is rarely the constraint to pollution control. The growth of pollution control services has been very pronounced in industrialized countries. For example in the U.S.A. the total expenditure for pollution control in 1979 was about US$56 billion, more than 2 percent of GNP. By 1988 this is expected to rise to US$160 billion. In Japan the investment in anti-pollution measures increased from about US$12 billion in 1970 to US$64 billion in 1975 and now averages US$30 billion per year.

Recently there has been an increase in the use of low and non-waste technologies in industry to encourage production with less and less dangerous waste, with raw materials and energy used more economically, and less-polluting end products.

Economic and fiscal measures are also being used to encourage environmental management and discourage pollution. These include tax rebates or subsidies for pollution-control equipment or the application of the Polluter Pays Principle adopted by OECD countries.

The needs for tomorrow

With population growth there will be more people with increasing aspirations for higher standards of living and an improved quality of life. The demand for natural resources and environmental amenities will increase accordingly and so will the potential impacts on environmental quality, if appropriate policies and strategies are not enacted. The challenge will be to meet these expectations while ensuring that the functioning and integrity of the ecosystem, particularly the critical life-support systems, are not irreversibly damaged.

There is now a growing acceptance of the concept of sustainable development as a means to meet this challenge, and the measures that need to be taken.

The Ministries and Departments of the Environment that have been established need strengthening. Many of them are relatively new, and resources — financial and personal — commensurate to the task, should be made available. The trend in an increasing number of countries which require development activities to be subject to an environmental impact assessment (EIA) process needs to be emulated in those countries which do not. Equally important is the establishment of policy directives to ensure that the EIA process be applied at the earliest feasible planning stage of any project, rather than when designs are completed and construction begins, when any changes will be time-consuming, costly and often unfeasible. The early application of the process will promote and facilitate the adoption of alternate sites, raw material use, manufacturing processes, products and such, with less impact on the environment and more efficient use of natural resources. To date, while the EIA process has been increasingly applied, it has been primarily aimed at the project level. To ensure the maximum effect it should be directed at the programme and planning levels as well.

The development plans of a country are generally based on economic parameters and indicators such as GNP and GDP. The wealth of a country is now measured by the quantity of minerals, fossil fuels, industrial and agricultural outputs. To promote sustainable development there is a need to apply the concept of "environmental accounting" as proposed by Dr. M. K. Tolba, the Executive Director of UNEP. This makes the quality of the water and air, the amount of top soil, the area of biosphere reserves needed for genetic diversity, and other ecological factors part of a country's patrimony.

When environmental institutions were established 10 to 15 years ago by a majority of countries, the major focus was on pollution control, since pollutants from industry, transportation and homes were visibly a cause of environmental degradation. Now, however, there is a growing recognition that this is not enough. There is also a need to consider preventive measures in the use of resources and the secondary and tertiary impacts of environmental degredation, particularly those affecting social and cultural conditions. There is an imperative need for an integrated approach to ensure that the people who are trained in pollution control are also educated in the broader aspects of environmental management. Without them it will not be possible to conceive, plan and implement the integration of environmental considerations for sustainable development.

While countries have enacted environmental legislation, it has not yet been vigorously enforced due to lack of personnel, finances and information on the most cost-effective solutions. These constraints are most prevalent in developing countries. Greater enforcement, therefore, should be accompanied by incentives and assistance to encourage adoption of environmental management.

During the past two decades the public has been provided with accounts of the extent of the degradation of planet earth. They must continue to be supplied with credible information. This should include reports on the increasing number of activities that are being undertaken to improve the state of the environment, to show that solutions can be found, so that people do not feel hopeless and despondent.

There is a recognition that for any activity to yield maximum benefits there must be a focus at grass-root levels. There must be people participation with a strategy that accepts the role of the individual.

The attitudes and actions of a person can have very important impacts on environmental quality and natural resource use, as an example for others. So can the sum of individual attitudes and actions have a very telling impact. Hence it is imperative to motivate and orient all people, most specifically the individual, to place a higher premium on ethical values. Compassion and tolerance towards all living beings; respect for all forms of life; harmony with nature rather than the arrogance to conquer it; responsible stewardship of nature for the benefits of present and future generations; less profligate use of resources — these are some of the fundamental attitudes and practices that need to be strengthened.

The Lord Buddha recognised these ethical principles and taught and practiced them Himself over two millennia ago. These principles apply even more today. The need for today and tomorrow is for the individual to be aware of the fundamental importance of environmental ethics and practice them.

Nay Htun, Ph.D., a Buddhist, is Regional Director and Representative for Asia and the Pacific of the United Nations Environment Programme. Prior to joining UNEP in 1976, he was Professor of Environmental Engineering at the Asian Institute of Technology as well as working for a multinational energy company. His contribution here is written in a personal capacity.

References

Brown, L.R. and others (1986). State of the World. A Worldwatch Institute Report on Progress Towards a Sustainable Society, W.W. Norton & Company, New York, London.

United Nations Environment Programme, UNEP (1982). The World Environment 1972-1982. Ed. by M.W. Holdgate, M. Kassas, G.F. White. United Nations Environment Programme.

UNEP/WMO/ICSU (1985). An Assessment of the Role of Carbon Dioxide and other Greenhouse Gases in Climate Variations and Associated Impacts. WMO, Geneva.

UNEP (1986). Directory of Tertiary Level Institutions Offering Environmental Education and Training Courses in Asia and Pacific Region. UNEP Regional Office for Asia and the Pacific, Bangkok.

World Resources Institute (1986). An Assessment of the Resource Base that Supports the Global Economy. Basic Books Inc., New York.

THE BUDDHIST PERCEPTION OF NATURE PROJECT

By Nancy Nash

"The world grows smaller and smaller, more and more interdependent ... today more than ever before life must be characterised by a sense of Universal Responsibility, not only nation to nation and human to human, but also human to other forms of life."

— His Holiness the XIV Dalai Lama

Buddhist Perception of Nature, established in 1985 to help improve awareness, attitudes, and actions to protect the natural environment, took root with this statement by His Holiness the Dalai Lama during the course of an interview in 1979, and has been nurtured at every step with inspiration and support from the world's foremost Buddhist, one of the world's greatest spiritual leaders.

Being in the presence or simply reading and absorbing the works of this extraordinary teacher is always a lesson in compassion for all life, whatever the subject — and His Holiness's range is universal. A memorable gathering of representatives of Christianity, Hinduism, Islam and Judaism in honour of this Buddhist monk, in the Swiss city of Geneva in 1988, illustrates. Each claimed as the best of his own different faith, the lessons in loving kindness including for the earth itself and all living beings, of the Dalai Lama of Tibet.

That event became one of the cornerstones of Buddhist Perception of Nature outreaches and companion projects with other religions and cultural traditions that would expand and enrich ecumenical work for environmental ethics. But the main objective at the start was researching, assembling, and putting to use as educational tools, Buddhist teachings about humankind's responsibilities to the natural world.

Many of the lessons from the faith's literature and traditions date back more than 2,500 years. But as Sir Peter Scott, one of the world's greatest naturalists, and among the first people to endorse this project, points out in ***TREE Of LIFE***'s Introduction, they are as valid today as they have ever been, and capable of reaching out in contemporary society to bring about urgently needed conservation.

When Sir Peter died in 1989, he left a rich legacy of humanitarian endeavour — accomplishments in art and sport, appreciation of music shared with others as a teaching tool, and love of nature and a pioneering role in creating international institutions dedicated to protection of all life on earth. His greatest gift to future generations, however, may have been his model of holism in conservation, embracing as integrated rather than separate elements, nature and culture.

Buddhism in fact, was selected with Sir Peter's enthusiastic support as a pilot project in new perspectives for conservation because education is identified as the most important element in long-term success, and the power of religious and spiritual faith for the most part had been missing from the international environmental protection movement at that time.

With this ancient, enduring philosophy, themes of awareness and compassion for all life are deeply embodied. Here also is a religion influential in many parts of Asia with its rich, unique and all too often endangered species of animals, plants, habitats and ecosystems — perhaps the greatest treasurehouse of biodiversity on the planet — and with a demonstrated, direct beneficial effect in saving some known major threatened species of wildlife and habitats. The faith's traditions in art, architecture, literature and music are among important aspects of the world's heritage, and blend conservation of both culture and nature.

The Tibetan Buddhist leader-monk-saint and the British artist-athlete-naturalist, the two people most responsible for inspiring Buddhist Perception of Nature, met only once, but in an atmosphere of great warmth and instant brotherhood. Ideas exchanged naturally embraced spirituality, but surprisingly for a handful of listeners, became most lively on the theme of science, which they both recognised as a vital inseparable part of human cultures, and — employed ethically — a valuable tool for protection of nature. Our project recognises that science is essential, first to set priorities for the work, and to persuade educated leaders and decision-makers. Then our best scientific minds are needed to help rectify the ecological disasters we face resulting from ignorance, greed, and lack of respect for life on earth.

Scientific experts are the first professionals to point out that the earth's capacity to support life is being reduced at the time it is needed most — as rising human numbers, expectations, and consumption make increasingly heavy demands. But science outlines the state of the earth to the best of our knowledge. Religion and cultural traditions are the repositories of human values, which among many other things, decides how knowledge is used.

The twain can meet and have done with Buddhist Perception of Nature. Among the first people to come forward with help was world-famous wildlife biologist Dr. George B. Schaller, who supported the premise that only with aroused personal and social values that embrace compassion for fellow beings and generosity for nature that is so generous to us, can we deal successfully with problems threatening survival of life on earth as we know it.

The conservation effect in the Buddhist world until recently has been described as positive, but passive. Animals inhabiting the grounds of temples, for example, have automatic sanctuary for Buddhist faithful; in Thailand rules for monks living in forest monasteries are so strict that their areas are naturally rich in natural health and well cared for. Tibet, by all accounts, until the Buddhist culture was severely disrupted by the Chinese takeover 50 years ago, was a land where people and wildlife lived together in extraordinary harmony, where even landscapes were considered sacred.

The environmental crisis we face today, however, needs active help, and the world's estimated 600 million Buddhists can make a major positive impact by becoming dynamic conservationists. That can only come about by sincerely employing the faith's teachings. The importance of excellence in scholarship cannot be over-estimated in a project of this kind, and we have been fortunate that, from the commencement of work, research has been under the direction of highly respected institutions, and carried out by superb scholars.

The Council for Religious and Cultural Affairs and the Department of Information and International Relations of His Holiness the Dalai Lama have provided direction for Mahayana studies. For Theravada traditions, work was first guided by Wildlife Fund Thailand in association with experts from the Thai Ministry of Education, and Thammasat University.

The project's first chief scholars are as exceptional as the work they undertook. Venerable Karma Gelek Yuthok, then based at the School of Dialectics in Dharamsala, headquarters of the Tibetan Government-in-Exile, now heads The Office of Tibet in Japan. Dr. Chatsumarn Kabilsingh, of the Faculty of Liberal Arts, Thammasat University in Bangkok, is such a widely respected authority on Buddhism in Thailand, she was every expert's first choice. These two representatives of Buddhism's branches in the ***TREE Of LIFE*** and their colleagues assisting with research, compiling and translating, did a remarkable launch of the work, involving a vast literature and history, in a very short space of time.

Kasur Lodi Gyaltsen Gyari, Tibetan Coordinator for the project and its international outreaches, first undertook this work as Deputy Minister for Education in His Holiness the Dalai Lama's Kashag (Cabinet) in Dharamsala, and continues as Kasur — Special Envoy of the Dalai Lama — based in Washington D C.

At the formal start of Buddhist Perception of Nature in 1985, and for the first three ground-breaking years, like Lodi Gyari for the Tibetans, Khun Sirajit Waramontri was Thai Coordinator. Both team leaders and their remarkable teams have given valuable time, energy, and talent to pioneer the work and keep it going with momentum resulting in, for example, both the establishment of an ecology department — popularly called "Eco-Desk" — within the Tibetan Government-in-Exile in Dharamsala, India, and of Buddhism and Nature Protection in Thailand (BNPT).

BNPT has produced many teaching aids, including *A CRY FROM THE FOREST* in English and Thai, and in Thai, the first ever nature protection-focused Buddhist book for use in Thailand's more than 35,000 temples throughout the country — an extraordinary breakthrough in a nation where much primary education starts with religious teachings in sacred surroundings. The Dharamsala-based Tibetan Eco-Desk and Tibet support groups around the world have been equally dedicated in researching, writing and publishing books and periodicals focused on the importance of conservation of nature, and of great value to scientific and cultural integrity.

Documents made widely available for the first time included a Declaration on Protection of the Environment by the XIII Dalai of Tibet at the beginning of the century. Scholars and many other educated Tibetans knew about the proclamation, and most of the general population, devoutly Buddhist, were natural conservationists. But Thai and other Buddhist researchers, and those from other faiths collaborating, were fascinated that even the previous Dalai Lama was concerned with formal protection of nature — and at a stage of history few other spiritual or secular leaders anywhere addressed the subject, even though their own natural resources were already being seriously degraded.

Activities have included participation in the 1992 "Earth Summit" in Rio de Janeiro — where thousands of traditional Tibetan prayer flags printed with the Dalai Lama's Declaration on Environmental Ethics made up one of the most colourful and meaningful exhibits. Annual events such as Earth Day tree-planting and "clean-ups" now take place in exile Tibetan communities throughout India and elsewhere.

It is of very special note culturally, that at the start of Buddhist Perception of Nature Dr. Chatsumarn pointed out this collaboration to help protect nature and all life on earth has not only an urgent and important role in modern times, but historical significance as well. It is probably the first time in approximately 2000 years that Mahayana and Theravada scholars have worked together on such a goal.

Tibetan and Thai Buddhists undertook the initial work because they were sympathetic to the cause and willing to assume the burden of the tasks. Since then, contacts have been made with Buddhist scholars of scripture and history, and groups interested in spirituality and biology in more than 30 countries.

Because of the global concerns of conservation, this project from the beginning was envisioned first for Buddhists, but also as an adaptable blueprint for research and achievement for similar projects involving other faiths and cultural traditions. In this role, accomplishments have gone far beyond original expectations.

Buddhist Perception of Nature at the time of founding was already part of the International Union for Conservation of Nature and Natural Resources (IUCN) Working Group for Environmental Ethics, founded by Prof. J. Ronald Engel, another pioneer in this field we've been privileged to know.

Within the first year of operations there were contacts with Hindu, Moslem, Jewish and Christian individuals and groups, as well as many scientists not aligned with a particular faith but appreciating the endowment of spirituality in environmental protection. Within six months of the announcement of the project's 1987 Rolex Award, the "blueprint" project outline that had been envisioned as a secondary outreach, had been provided to researchers and scholars in more than a dozen countries.

To date, Buddhist Perception of Nature's teaching materials have been provided to nature clubs, colleges and universities, conservation groups and individuals, and libraries in more than 35 countries in Asia, Europe, Latin America, the Middle East, and Africa. ***TREE Of LIFE*** and other teaching tools are texts in use in ecology courses in a number of universities in Asia, the Americas, and Europe. The project and its theme of ethics has been a focal point in conferences internationally — including London, Mexico City, Chicago, Rio de Janeiro, Bangkok, Singapore, New York, Toronto, New Delhi, Rome, Hong Kong and Ulaan Baator.

His Holiness the Dalai Lama's Declaration on Environmental Ethics, dated 5 June 1986, in recognition of the United Nations Environment Programme (UNEP) World Environment Day and that year's theme, Peace and the Environment, has been translated into more than a dozen languages, and ***TREE Of LIFE*** in its entire first edition form into Chinese, German, and Spanish. In 1993, Buddhist Perception of Nature was added to UNEP's Global 500 Roll of Honour.

The importance of the inspiration, endorsement and support of the Dalai Lama is impossible to overestimate. His teachings, willingness to take on duty and responsibility, and ability to attract and enlist awareness and support from other spiritual and political leaders around the world has been one of the many blessings not only our project, but also the world, has received

Everyone involved with and touched by this work, has surely gained some knowledge and compassion for all life forms. We hope that Buddhist Perception of Nature is not only a viable response of the many needed to help solve the earth's ecological problems, but also an element in a much needed renaissance of environmental and all other fields of ethics. It is fitting in this present edition to finish with a statement on the presentation to His Holiness the Dalai Lama of Tibet of the 1989 Nobel Peace Prize:

> ***"...the Dalai Lama in his struggle for the liberation of Tibet consistently has opposed the use of violence. He has instead advocated peaceful solutions based upon tolerance and mutual respect in order to preserve the historical and cultural heritage of his people. The Dalai Lama has developed his philosophy from a great reverence for all things living and upon the concept of Universal Responsibility embracing all mankind as well as nature. In the opinion of the committee, the Dalai Lama has come forward with constructive and forward-looking proposals for the solution of international conflicts, human rights issues, and global environmental problems."***

Nancy Nash, originator and international coordinator of Buddhist Perception of Nature, is an American, a Christian, and author of more than 100 magazine and book articles and chapters about nature conservation, wildlife, and culture.

APPENDIX I

Alliance of Religions and Conservation (ARC)
3 Wynnstay Grove
Fallowfield, Manchester M14 6XG, UK
Tel: 44 (0)161 248 5731
Fax: 44 (0)161 248 5736
e-mail: icorec@icorec.nwnet.co.uk

Assisi Nature Council
3 Avenue de Jaman
1005 Lausanne, Switzerland
Tel: 41 (0)21 320 7043
Fax: 41 (0)21 320 0736
e-mail: edet@assisiinc.ch

Au Sable Institute of Environmental Studies
6526 Sunset Tr. N E
Mancelona, MI 49659, USA
Tel: 1 608 222 1139
email: MJAuSable@aol.com
http://www.ausable.org

Buddhism and Nature Protection in Thailand
c/o Dr. Chatsumarn Kabilsingh
Faculty of Liberal Arts,
Thammasat University
Bangkok 10200, Thailand
Tel/Fax: 662 221 6171-80 ext. 1218
e-mail: kabil@alpha.tu.ac.th

Buddhist Publication Society
P O Box 61, #54 Sangharaja, Mawata
Kandy, Sri Lanka

Clean Up The World
18 Bridge Road
Glebe, Sydney NSW 2037
Australia
Tel: 612 9629 0700
Fax: 612 9692 0761
e-mail: world@cleanup.com.au
http://www.cleanuptheworld.org.au

Council on the Sustainable Development of Central Asia (CoDoCa)
P O Box 347, 1400 AH Bussum
The Netherlands
Tel: 31 35 693 4266
Fax: 31 35 693 5254
e-mail: 101651.1370@compuserve.com
http://ourworld.compuserve.com/home pages/codoca

Environment Desk
Dept. Of Information and International Relations
Gangchen Kyishong
176215 Dharamsala, H. P., India
Tel: 91 1892 22510
Fax: 91 1892 24957
e-mail: ecodesk@tcrclinuxernet.in
(Green Tibet 1997 and 1998, and the ECODESK brochure
are available on the internet on
http://www.tibet.com)

IUCN Ethics Working Group
Commission on Environmental Law
c/o Strachen Donnelley, Director
Program on Humans Nature
The Hastings Center for Bioethics
Garrison 10524-5555, New York, USA

IUCN the World Conservation Union
Rue Mauverney 28
CH-1196 Gland, Switzerland
Tel: 41 22 999 0001
Fax: 41 22 999 0002
e-mail: mail@hq.iucn.ch
http://www.iucn.org

World Wide Fund for Nature (WWF) International
Avenue du Mont-Blanc
CH-1196 Gland, Switzerland
Tel: 41 22 364 9111
Fax: 41 22 364 5358
http://www.panda.org

World Conservation Monitoring Centre
219 Huntingdon Road
Cambridge CB3 ODL, England, U K
Tel: 44 1223 277314
Fax: 44 1223 277136
e-mail: info@wcmc.org.uk
http://www.wcmc.org.uk

World Resources Institute (WRI)
1709 New York Ave. N W
Washington D C 20006
Tel: 1 202 638 6300
Fax: 1 202 638 0036
website (updated daily): www.wri.org
info by e-mail: lauralee@wri.com

United Nations Development Programme (UNDP)
United Nations Plaza
New York 10017, New York, USA
Tel: 1 212 906 5000
http://www.undp.org

United Nations Environment Programme (UNEP)
P O Box 30552
Nairobi, Kenya
Tel: 2542 621 234
Fax: 2542 623 927
"Our Planet" http://www.ourplanet.com

APPENDIX II

A vast reservoir of important sources of information and inspiration for environmental ethics and protection work now exists and is constantly growing. Added to books, still the greatest mine of material, are now many films, documentaries and websites, conferences that produce much needed updates in thoughtful presentations, and events of exhibition and performance art.

Buddhist Perception of Nature's research bibliography features more than 1,000 entries, some with dozens of lines each. It's not possible in this little volume to publish even the list of titles and our special anthology as well. Decisions about what to include from all of the world's incredibly rich literature related to our subject have been debated, reviewed again and again, sought recommendations, and debated again.

The resulting collection of works presented is not the newest or by any means the largest of its kind. But it is a little treasure we're happy to share, composed of only some of the many, many other jewels we would have loved to include. In the space available, it was also decided to incorporate an informal Recommended Reading — again far from complete, but presented here to highlight some of the major works and their authors inspiring or involved with all manner of ongoing research and achievements for environmental ethics.

Chatsumarn Kabilsingh's latest book we include with great pleasure: *BUDDHISM AND NATURE PROTECTION*, published in Thailand at the same time this second edition of work we did together goes to press in Hong Kong. Her earlier book with Sirajit Waramontri is the beautiful *A CRY FROM THE FOREST*.

An impressive list of publications appears regularly from the Environment Dept. of the Tibetan Government-in-Exile in India. *HIS HOLINESS THE DALAI LAMA ON ENVIRONMENT*, a tree-planting ceremony on the cover, is much appreciated in many libraries, as is *MY TIBET* (U of California Press) with Galen Rowell, in photos and text depicting the land as sacred, where, as His Holiness says, "in the majestic beauty of Tibet's natural surroundings, the people developed their culture."

Thai pioneer of conservation Boonsong Lekagul, who died just as Buddhist Perception of Nature came to life in ways that he helped so much bring about, is listed in Acknowledgments, but that falls far short of even beginning to recognise properly his special role in this work. Like Peter Scott, a contemporary Renaissance Man interested in everything from Art to Zoology, his contributions saved much that would have been otherwise already lost in Southeast Asia. It says much of both men that when Boonsong received a special WWF award in 1979, some called him "The Sir Peter of Thailand", but Scott said he would be proud to be called the "Dr. Boonsong of the UK". The great literary output of both men, often illustrated with their own art, is highly recommended and will find a special place in every environmentalist's heart.

The Renaissance Woman closest to our hearts — and the centre of our project's goals and achievements — is Fleur Cowles. As artist, writer, editor and lifestyle trend-setter who embraced importance of protection of nature long before it became fashionable, she in fact helped bring environment into vogue. Her famous tigers and wildlife paintings and illustrations for prize-winning books such as *TIGER FLOWER* and *LION AND BLUE* linked children and adults in appreciation of stunning fantasy based on even more beautiful wildlife reality. An original, one many of her admirers have titled Tigress in Defense of Nature, every book she has written, illustrated or been associated with is a treasure.

Wildlife biologist George Schaller is another original, combining strict science — studies of the mountain gorilla, tiger, giant panda and other large mammals stand as the first of depth and substance — along with adventure-filled travels, and sensitivity to every encounter, be it a vast landscape or small-minded bureaucrat, delicate common flowers or a rare animal in the wild. His books have engaged a wide popular audience with a shared sense of rapture about wild nature and its vital importance, a sense of shame about what humankind has done to irreplaceable living species and their habitats, and a determination to save from extinction what remains. *TIBET'S HIDDEN WILDERNESS* (Abrams, 1997) is the most recent in a long list of recommended Schaller reading.

In the same spirit of important work that has captured a large following for wildlife conservation are works by Joy Adamson on lions, Jane Goodall on primates, Richard O'Barry on dolphins, Iain and Oria Douglas-Hamilton on elephants, Esmond and Chrysse Bradley-Martin on rhinos, and Pierre Pfeffer in French, and Gerald Durrell in English on explorations in Asia and Africa, and many furred, feathered and scaled creatures, and even "creepy-crawlies" as insects are affectionately known. Environmental ethics also embraces humane conditions and treatment of domestic animal life, and Tom Regan, Michael Fox, Cleveland Amory and Konrad Lorenz have produced classic texts in this field.

Laurens Van Der Post, honoured with many titles including a knighthood shortly before his death, bestowed on the world a great body of work. Covering so many places, cultures, events and schools of thought, often — as with the Kalahari explorations — the first writer ever to do so, always with fresh insights and the greatest sensitivity, one is filled with admiration that one man accomplished so much, and so much that is valuable and enduring, in one lifetime. All of his books have enriched Buddhist Perception of Nature research and thought, but special mention should be made of The *SEED AND THE SOWER*, and *JUNG AND THE STORY OF OUR TIME.*

As a teacher who is also a genuine educator, a guide of budding minds who encourages creative new branches in what we'll call the Tree of Philosophy, Steven C. Rockefeller stands out. Among his achievements, two extraordinary conferences he conceived and led in the carrying out at Middlebury College, Vermont, and their published results under the same titles have been entwined with Buddhist Perception of Nature's own love of knowledge — and positive action. *THE CHRIST AND THE*

BODHISATTVA in 1984 helped inspire our project. More recently, *SPIRIT AND NATURE* involved our progress, and like the earlier gathering, was blessed with the presence of His Holiness the Dalai Lama.

Ronald Engel's chapter in *SPIRIT AND NATURE* articulates so splendidly the breakthroughs needed in linking practical and moral issues, every student of these subjects should find it required reading. A focus on environmental ethics has been Engel's main work; few have contributed as much major thought and literature in this field, and none better. His award-winning *SACRED SANDS* was summed up in a review in American Studies as a "rare combination of environmental science, political process and religious symbolism..."

Many fundamental books, such as *SILENT SPRING*, Aldo Leopold's *THE LAND ETHIC*, *REVERENCE FOR LIFE* and many other works of Albert Schweitzer, even the extraordinary writings of Meister Eckhart 600 years ago, emerged this century and became widely known in the Western world, now called in geopolitical terms the North, generally to contrast, wherever the location on the globe, the "developed" from the "developing or so-called under-developed", so-called South. The relatively materially richer North for a start generally allows more freedom from struggle to simply survive and therefore the opportunity to produce thoughtful works on the subject, and other freedoms — of thought, speech and publication.

Any perceived cultural bias in the extensive use of English in the work comes about not always by choice, but owing to the fact more original and translated sources are accessible in English than any other language. Deliberate bias and inequities largely arising from greed, but to be fair, also ignorance, do exist in the world to a degree that cries out for improved ethics in all elements of human life, often starting with the natural environment.

Lewis Regenstein's *AMERICA THE POISONED* and *THE POLITICS OF EXTINCTION* are among the best reports covering the modern map of exploitation, starting with the European colonisation of the Americas and including that of the unethical powerful over the powerless anywhere this occurs. David Korten has devoted a life's work to exposing economic imperialism — the North's exploitation of resources of the South being a prime, ugly example — and describing what that means for global natural resources and general human health and progress from village to national levels; his most recent book is *THE POST-CORPORATE WORLD*.

Even within the congenial conservation community, marine biologist Sylvia Earle must constantly fight in her gentle, eloquent voice, in scientific articles, speeches, and books including *EXPLORING THE DEEP FRONTIER* (National Geographic Society) for oceans and seas, the earth's "lungs", and their rich, largely unknown life, to receive at least the same attention as terrestrial life. Insects and micro-organisms, essential to life on earth, have few high-profile spokesmen aside from E. O. Wilson, but there couldn't be better; his *BIOPHILIA* is one of the jewels we would have loved to reproduce here, in full.

Peter Raven, a star in the conservation firmament, fights for survival, health and biological diversity of the plant world — on which all life on earth depends — and it's been said of his *BIOLOGY OF PLANTS* that if only one major book on biology altogether were allowed to a reader, this is the one of greatest value.

IUCN, UNDP, UNEP, WCMC, WRI and WWF, all listed in Appendix I, are sources the world depends on for updated information, best as available and possible to disseminate about earth's environment globally. And they in turn depend on the dedicated work of individual experts, some already acknowledged in ***TREE Of LIFE***, but with special mention here of Mostafa Tolba's extraordinary and courageous articles, speeches and books. Additional special names to look for include Ali Amer Al-Kiyumi, Esmond Bradley-Martin, Lee Talbot, Lester Brown, Thomas Lovejoy, Norman Myers, and many others we regret not being able to list.

Thomas Berry in many writings but especially *THE DREAM OF THE EARTH*, Brian Swimme with *THE EARTH IS A GREEN DRAGON*, and *THE UNIVERSE STORY* these two great thinkers worked on together, made important breakthroughs in cosmology and brought new energy to examination of the entire universe and the laws which govern it as a whole. It's not possible, given this informal Recommended Reading, to provide an environmental ethics map showing where the literature and learning of cosmology and biology, religion and spirituality, modern science and cultural traditions, and much more that is involved converge, or meet and branch out. The map in any case is never the actual territory, and nothing less than an encyclopedia would be adequate for the work by those in many parts of the world, in many languages, most sincerely doing the jobs. But it is vital to emphasise that works by Berry and Swimme are considered bedrock essential reading.

IUCN, UNEP and WWF in 1980 announced the world's first *WORLD CONSERVATION STRATEGY* — the result of years of study and input from experts around the world — followed up just over a decade later by *CARING FOR THE EARTH*. The texts of both documents are valuable and still in use. The Future Generations Network (U of Malta) began publishing a Journal of great importance to ethics around the same time UNEP in 1990 produced *ONLY ONE EARTH*, a lovely event celebrating Environmental Sabbath and a publication that included declarations on human stewardship of nature from five of the world's major religions.

The same year, *STATE OF THE WORLD* by the Worldwatch Institute set a new standard of "no punches pulled" reporting. Although *CARING FOR THE FUTURE*, a report of the Independent Commission on Population and Quality of Life, with authors from 20 countries under the direction of Maria de Lourdes Pintasilgo, appeared quite recently (1996), it earned admiration and joined the impressive literature that has unquestionably influenced governments. National leaders respecting public opinion are finally beginning to catch up with the cause — and the groundswell of demands for better protection of nature from a growing number of their fellow citizens.

But as recently as 1985, when Japanese Prime Minister Yasuhiro Nakasone, in his address at the 40th anniversary of the United Nations, made a reasoned yet passionate plea for "a new global ethic" and urgent reversal of destruction of our planet, it was such an outstanding breakthrough for a politician, ***TREE Of LIFE*** (1987) published the full environment portion of the text. Our second edition does so again.

In 1987, *OUR COMMON FUTURE* by Gro Harlem Brundtland, for the World Commission on Environment and Development, focused even more global — and political — attention on conservation's grave problems and possible solutions. When Mikhail Gorbachev addressed the Global Forum on Human Survival in Mosow in 1990, his topic was "The Ecological Imperative". Al Gore's *EARTH IN THE BALANCE*, published in 1992 when he was a U.S. Senator, is a major addition to the literature, filled with hard-hitting facts presented with an elegant humanitarianism summed up in the book's subtitle: *Ecology and the Human Spirit.*

Public awareness of the importance of nature has increased greatly, even though many people are still only concerned about their immediate surroundings, not realising that whatever happens throughout the biosphere impacts on all life. Therefore, it takes tremendous courage on the part of a leader to fully commit a nation to strict policies that not only include protection of wild flora and fauna throughout a country, but also even migratory species.

Such a leader is H.M. Qaboos bin Said, Sultan of Oman, who has guided one of the most backward countries in the world 25 years ago into one of the most progressive anywhere today, hugely increasing the quality of human life without sacrificing the highest principles of conservation. Reports of scientific expeditions published by the Diwan of Royal Court make wonderful reading, for the fascinating information on a little known country and their inspiring messages, based on deep religious faith, from the country's enlightened pilot. Sultan Qaboos, whose dedication to conservation extends beyond Oman's borders, among many international good works, is largely responsible establishing The Peter Scott Memorial, administered by the Species Survival Commission, UK, and the Indian Ocean Blue Whale Sanctuary.

Gaia theory, Deep Ecology philosophy, and Christian theologically based studies often under the heading Cosmic Christ are some of the widely recognised, great new-thinking intellectual paths that help make environmental ethics work so spiritually alive and vibrant, and thanks go to James Lovelock, Arne Naess, Matthew Fox, and others including Lyall Watson for *SUPERNATURE* and *GIFTS Of UNKNOWN THINGS.* Leading thinkers producing educational materials under the specific heading Environmental Ethics start with Holmes Rolston, Kristin Schrader-Frechette, and Laura Westra.

International and regional conferences on every topic from political, military and economic alliances to seminars on every human subject of study under the sun almost always include now the need for respect for the natural environment in their published conclusions, and these nuggets make fascinating reading in context.

The word "declare" embraces such a wide range of alternate meanings, it is easy to see why a formal Declaration may admit and confess, announce and notify, claim, certify and swear, plead or insist, testify and vow — depending on the "voice", some or all of that and more. Whether the work of individuals, nations, or international institutions, the result of a single deep meditation or months and years of global input, bargaining and negotiating, when these documents about nature and our earth are issued officially they are usually poetic.

Earth, the only home all living things know, is being destroyed. Nature, essential for all life on earth, the inspiration for the greatest arts and indeed the source of most artists' materials, is rapidly being diminished. Extinction is forever. Future generations will inherit far less than current generations have enjoyed, and largely plundered. These elements in contemplating statements of faith that we can do better, and the intention to do so, shed rhetoric and animate genuine spirituality and eloquence.

The Dalai Lama's Declaration on Environmental Ethics mentions neither religion nor spirituality but is permeated with a sense of scared responsibility. The 1982 Gubbio Declaration, commemorating the 800th anniversary of the birth of St. Francis, is a deeply moving document in defense of the the earth and all living things. The United Nations Conference on Environment and Development resulted in the unprecedented Agenda 21, ratified by 178 nations; UNEP produced an anthology of associated ETHICS literature. The Baha'i' Statement on Nature published in 1987 has become a classic text, as has The Chipko Message in the same year, arising from one of the most inspiring and broad-based grassroots movements in the world, and these outstanding examples only begin the list.

Anthologies of formal declarations are appearing regularly, along with reprints of small volumes that are perennials and it starts with an important video narrated by Dr. Michael W. Fox, for the Centre for Respect of Life and Environment based in Washington DC: *ANIMALS, NATURE AND RELIGION. HOLY GROUND: The Guide to Faith and Ecology* (1997, ARC) is one of the most recent and comprehensive, "must reading" for religious attitudes toward conservation, and based on two extraordinary conferences — Assisi in 1986, and Windsor in 1995.

Noted here are just a few found of importance in the Buddhist Perception of Nature library: *The Trees' Birthday* by Tu B'Sh'vat Haggadah; *A Sustainable Earth*; *Religion and Ecology in the Western Hemisphere* by Calvin B. DeWitt; *Technology and the Healing of the Earth* by Thomas Berry; *Replenish the Earth: the Bible's Message of Conservation and Kindness to Animals* by the Interfaith Council for the Protection of Animals and Nature; and *Religion, Nature and Survival* by the Inter-Religious Forum For Community Harmony. Finally, in a class of its own is a simple, eight word call for action summing up so much of the spiritual impetus needed in the work. It is a line from The Mandate for Life on Earth, which has been signed by millions of people of all ages around the world: Let's move the World to save the Earth.

"We need a boundless ethic which will include the animals also."

Albert Schweitzer
quoted on the Animal Welfare Institute (U.S.) Medal
awarded annually since 1954

"The conservation of the environment is the responsibility of us all — a responsibility that knows no political boundaries."

H.M. Qaboos Bin Said, Sultan of Oman
in his message to The Earth Summit, 1992

"The earth is at the same time mother, she is mother of all that is natural, mother of all that is human. She is mother of all, for contained in her are the seeds of all."

Hildegard of Bingen
12th century Benedictine Abbess

The earth, its life am I, The earth, its feet are my feet, The earth, its legs are my legs, The earth, its body is my body, The earth, its thoughts are my thoughts, The earth, its's speech is my speech.

Navajo Chant

"The Hindu tradition of reverence for nature and all forms of life, vegetable or animal, represents a powerful tradition which needs to be re-nurtured and re-applied in our contemporary context."

Dr. Karan Singh
excerpt from the Hindu Declaration, Assisi, 1986

"Let us hope a day will dawn when the great religious teachings may at last begin to bear fruit; when we shall see the start of a new era, when man accords to animals the respect and status they have long deserved and for so long have been denied."

Al-Hafiz B. A. Masri
in his book, *ISLAMIC CONCERN FOR ANIMALS*, 1987

"His Holiness the Pope John Paul II and His Holiness the XIVth Dalai Lamamet this morning in the Vatican for about 30 minutes. This was the fifth meeting between the two spiritual leaders, who discussed today their deep commitment to world peace, spiritual values, and protection of the earth's natural environment.

In continuation of previous discussions, they further explored ways in which religion can help achieve these goals, through education, prayer, the practice of altruism and fostering a sense of universal responsibility.

His Holiness the Dalai Lama informed His Holiness the Pope of his new proposal for implementing his peace initiative for Tibet. Their Holinesses prayed for a better understanding of peoples for each other, protection of the earth and for world peace."

Joint Statement
after the visit of His Holiness the XIV Dalai Lama
to His Holiness the Pope John Paul II,
Rome, 14 June 1988

"Extinction is a difficult concept to grasp. It is an eternal concept. It's not at all like the killing of individual life forms that can be renewed through normal processes of reproduction. Nor is it simply diminishing numbers. Nor is it damage that can somehow be remedied or for which some substitute can be found. Nor is it something that simply affects our own generation."

Thomas Berry
on massive extinction of species,
THE DREAM OF THE EARTH, 1988

"We not only live on the earth but also are of the earth, and the thought of its death, or even of its mutilation, touches a deep chord in our nature."

Jonathan Schell
THE FATE OF THE EARTH, 1982

"Highest good is like water. Because water excels in benefiting the myriadcreatures without contending with them."

Lao Tzu (5th century B.C., China)

"In response to growing ecological destruction, a groundswell of public opinion is saying with one voice: we will not abandon our descendants to our ecological wasteland."

Mostafa K. Tolba
OUR RESPONSIBILITIES TO FUTURE GENERATIONS

"My little sisters, the birds, much bounden are ye unto God, your Creator, and always in every place ought ye to praise Him, for that He hath given you liberty to fly about everywhere, and hath also given you double and triple raiment; moreover He preserved your seed in the Ark of Noah, that your race might not perish out of the world; still more are ye beholden to Him for the element of the air which he hath appointed for you; beyond all this, ye sow not,neither do you reap; and God feedeth you, and giveth you the streams and fountains for your drink; the mountains and the valleys for your refuge and the high trees whereon to make your nests; and because ye know not how to spin or sew, God clotheth you, you and your children; wherefore your creator loveth you much, seeing that He hath bestowed on you so many benefits; and therefore, my little sisters, beware of the sin of ingratitude, and study always to give praises unto God."

St. Francis of Assisi (1182 – 1226)
SERMON TO THE BIRDS

"How can you buy or sell the sky? The land? The idea is strange to us. If we do not own the freshness of the air and the sparkle of the water, how can you buy them? Every part of this earth is sacred to my people.

Every shining pine needle, every sandy shore, every mist in the dark woods, every meadow, every humming insect. All are holy in the memory and experience of my people. If we sell our land, remember that the air is precious to us, that the air shares its spirit with all the life it supports. The wind that gave our grandfather his first breath also received his last sigh. The wind also gives our children the spirit of life. So if we sell you our land, you must keep it apart and sacred, a place where man can go to taste the wind that is sweetened by the meadow flowers.

Will you teach your children what we have taught our children? That the earth is our mother? What befalls the earth befalls all the sons of the earth?

This we know: the earth does not belong to man, man belongs to the earth. All things are connected like the blood that unites us all. Man did not weave the web of life, he is merely a strand in it. Whatever he does to the web, he does to himself.

One thing we know: Our God is also your God. The earth is precious to Him, and to harm the earth is to heap contempt on its Creator."

Chief Seattle
in a letter to US President Franklin Pierce, 1855

"I love this beautiful world
Where everything lives happily,
Where cattle ad sheep graze.
Where streams flow
Where plants grow,
Where rain falls and sun shines,
Where everything serves its Creator.
Please save its beauty.
Please save our beautiful world.

Hycinth Semakaleng Matsela
17, Lesotho

There are no trees in my town.
They were uprooted by huge
Buildings.
There are no flowers outside
My house.
They were killed by cement.
There are no birds gathered
On my windows. They were
Turned away by smog.

Vania Tsigaridi
14, Greece

from *CRY FOR OUR BEAUTIFUL WORLD: Young People From Over 70 Nations Plead For The Survival Of Our Natural World*, edited by Helen Exley, 1985

"All living things share certain basic needs: space, oxygen, nutrients, a way to reproduce, appropriate temperatures within a narrow range. Our awareness that these necessities are common to most is relatively new, as is the perception that our well-being is linked to that of other life forms."

Sylvia Earle
EXPLORING THE DEEP FRONTIER, 1980

"Man was created by Nature but his hands and mind have changed the natural world, and in the process changed himself. The development of human intelligence, the accumulation of knowledge, the increases in social production and social needs, have all strengthened Man's ability to influence and control Nature. But his power to damage and destroy it has grown even greater."

Introduction to *NATURE CONSERVATION IN CHINA*
Beijing Natural History Museum, 1983

"Many people dismiss predictions of a planet soon with too many people and widespread starvation by saying, 'They (meaning scientists, I think) will find solutions'. I am a scientist, and I know other scientists. Not one of us can revive an extinct species. It is the extraordinary diversity of nature that gives mankind the greatest possible range of responses to coming stresses."

Boonsong Lekagul
ASIAWEEK, 1979

"As the 21st century approaches, the world is being impoverished as its most fundamental capital stock — its species, habitats and ecosystems — erodes. Not since the Cretaceous Era ended some 65 million years ago have losses been so rapid and great."

Forword to *KEEPING OPTIONS ALIVE: The Scientific Basis For Conserving Biodiversity*, WRI, 1989

"We have misread our mandate.....When God said, 'You shall have dominion,' He was calling on us to be a caretaker, a steward of the creation. A steward's role is to preserve, to restore and to heal. Stewards do not exercise control over things. Their sense of security does not come from being in control, but rather from taking care of other beings."

Jeremy Rifkin
DECLARATION OF A HERETIC

"Are we so deafened by the lure of transitory gain that we cannot hear the spirit of the trees appealing to us? Are we so enslaved by the marketplace as to pledge our souls and those who come after us to what we now consider as well-being.....What shall it profit us, as a nation or a dominion, if we balance the budget at the cost of the destruction of the earth beneath our feet?"

Richard St. Barbe Baker (1889 – 1982)

"There is no trifling with nature; it is always true, grave, and severe; it is always in the right, and the faults and errors fall to our share. It defies incompetency, but reveals its secrets to the competent, the truthful, and the pure. Nature is the living, visible garment of God."

Johann Wolfgang von Goethe (1749 – 1832)

"All nature is a vast symbolism; every material fact has sheathed within it a spiritual truth."

E. H. Chapin (1814 – 1880)

"In contemplation of created things, by steps we may ascend to God."

John Milton (1608 – 1674)

"...We must not prosper at the expense of poverty and constraint for our descendants. We ought to leave them a world that is not diminished in its richness. Development must be sustainable, or it is no more than a brief interlude between aeons of human misery."

Paul Harrison
on "ethics", in *THE THIRD REVOLUTION*, 1992

"When I walk by the peasants' woods which I have saved from cutting hands, I realise that the climate is to some extent in my own power, and that if in a thousand years human beings are to be happy, I too shall have had some small hand in it."

Anton Chekov
UNCLE VANYA, 1897

"Every sacred center is consecrated by a manifestation of the sacred in some part of the natural order. A tree, a stone, a person, a book, a moral commandment — some aspect of the ordinary world becomes the vehicle for a decisive revelation of the sacred. When this occurs, the object, person, or event functions as a symbol of reality beyond itself. It remains what it is as a part of the natural order, but at the same time, it points to and shares in an underlying structure of the world. In this way, each manifestation of the sacred serves as a paradigm of the nature of the universe. A tree, for example, when experienced as a manifestation of the sacred, discloses the world as a living totality....."

J. Ronald Engel
SACRED SANDS, 1983

"Our concept of God forbids the idea of a cheap creation, of a throwaway universe in which everything is expendable save human existence."

The Archbishop of Canterbury

"The earth is being stripped naked, abused, wounded and left to bleed to death."

Wangari Maathai
Founder, Green Belt Movement,
Kenya

speaking at the Global Forum of
Spiritual and Parliamentary Leaders on
Human Survival, Christ Church, Oxford
University, UK, 1988

"This globe of ours has been spinning in space for a very long time and it has been subjected to some fairly rough treatment. Temperatures have fallen to create ice-ages and risen to encourage dense vegetation. The moving of tectonic plates has changed the shapes of land and sea masses and it has been battered by meteorites from space. All these are natural phenomena, but the present situation is not due to any of these. The only significant factor that coincides with the deterioration of the planet's health over the last century is the dramatic increase in the world's human population, which began some 200 years ago. The key issue for the conservation of our natural environment is to find ways of protecting it from the consequences of the human explosion."

HRH The Prince Philip, Duke of Edinburgh
The Road From Assisi To Windsor *

"There are of course many approaches to environmental conservation and it is impossible and unnecessary for religious leaders to take on all of them. But it is indispensable for religions and religious leaders to identify a set of values which is needed as a foundation for our civilisation of tomorrow. Re-evaluation of spiritual values is the most important agenda for humanity."

Teruaki Kawai
The Healing Of The Earth *

"Perhaps this is the greatest thing that religions bring to the practice of conservation — hope. Hope that we can change, rediscover our truths and then journey on together, each in our own ways, but side by side, towards a world in which the whole of life is loved, respected and appreciated. For this is a truth that we all can find within our own traditions and even within our own hearts."

Martin Palmer
The Practice Of Conservation By Religions *

"We are convinced of the inestimable value of our respective traditions and of what they can offer to re-establish ecological harmony; but, at the same time, we are humble enough to desire to learn from each other. The very richness of our diversity lends strength to our shared concern and responsibility for our Planet Earth."

Father Serrini, Minister General of the Franciscans
The Assisi Declarations *

"Man's dominion cannot be understood as license to abuse, spoil, squander or destroy what God has made to manifest his glory. That dominion cannot be anything but a stewardship in symbiosis with all creatures."

From "Christianity", The Assisi Declarations *

"Allah is Unity; and His Unity is also reflected in the unity of humanity, and the unity of mankind and nature. His trustees are responsible for maintaining the unity of His creation, the integrity of the Earth, its flora and fauna, its wildlife and natural environment. Unity cannot be had by discord, by setting one need against another or letting one end predominate over another; it is maintained by balance and harmony."

From "Islam", The Assisi Declarations *

"Ahimsa (non-violence) is a principle that Jains teach and practise not only towards human beings but also towards all nature. It is an uneqivocal teaching that is at once ancient and contemporary..... Jain cosmology recognises the fundamental natural phenomenon of symbiosis or mutual dependence. All aspects of nature belong together and are bound is a physical as well as a metaphysical relationship. Life is viewed as a gift of togetherness, accommodation and assistance in a universe teeming with interdependent constituents"

From "Jainism", The Assisi Declarations *

"Having brought the world into being, God sustains, nourishes and protects it. Nothing is overlooked. Even creatures in rocks and stones are well provided for. Birds who fly thousands of miles away leaving their young ones behind know that they would be sustained and taught to fend for themselves by God (Guru Arjan, in Rehras). The creatures of nature lead their lives under God's command and with God's grace."

From "Sikhism", The Assisi Declarations *

"The natural harmony which should exist in the play of energies between humanity and the natural world is now disrupted by the weakest player in the game — humanity. Although it is the totality of this game that provides our nourishment, through ignorance of our own natural limits we destroy this source of nourishment."

Shrivatsa Goswami, (on "Hinduism"), Breaking The Family
The Windsor Statements *

"In light of the interdependence and reciprocity of all parts of nature, the evolutionary perfection of all beings, and the importance of diversity 'to the beauty, efficiency and perfection of the whole' (Abdu'l-Baha), it is clear to the Baha'is that, in the ordering of human affairs, every effort should be made to preserve as much as possible of the earth's biodiversity and natural order."

The Baha'i Teachings on Conservation
and Sustainable Development
The Windsor Statements *

"Three Jews, three opinions" — you laugh
Out of your modesty, relaxing the tension,
As the gift of your humour warms the air

And then the joke's on you, as your glasses
Slip briefly off your nose—
As you turn to gravity, to what matters here

And in that brief nakedness of your eyes
Everything you say resonates as it needs to, now

"Animals were not created to serve Man,
Nothing in Creation was created to serve Man,
We must change..."

As the green herb of Genesis drifts back
As you talk of the root we have ravaged and plucked
In the forests of our lungs and breathing —

"To create the land of milk and honey again
That the Bible so warmly promises..."
— oh song of songs, of flesh with flesh
And with grass and stone, as one,
Song of Songs sung into the wound —

Into the rape of our desecration...and now?

As you say it, it's not looking above, below, or back
But forward, into the sacred sign
You trace between your mouth and finger, raised

In a language so like Deaf and Dumb.

JUDAISM after Rabbi Arthur Hertzberg
by Jay Ramsay
The Windsor Statements *

"In order to protect the environment we must protect ourselves. We protect ourselves by opposing selfishness with generosity, ignorance with wisdom, and hatred with loving kindness. Selflessness, mindfulness, compassion and wisdom are the essence of Buddhism. We train in Buddhist meditation which enables us to be aware of the effects of our actions, including those destructive to our environment. Mindfulness and clear comprehension are at the heart of Buddhist meditation. Peace is realised when we are mindful of each and every step.

In the words of Maha Ghosananda: 'When we respect the environment, then nature will be good to us. When our hearts are good, then the sky will be good to us. The trees are like our mother and father, they feed us, nourish us, and provide us with everything; the fruit, leaves, the branches, the trunk. They give us food and satisfy many of our needs. So we spread the dharma (truth) of protecting ourselves and protecting our environment, which is the dharma of Buddha.'

.....In this universe of energies, everything affects everything else. Nature is an eco-system in which trees affect climate, the soil and the animals, just as the climate affects the trees, the soil, the animals . . . we are an intrinsic part of all existence . . . "

From "Buddhism", The Windsor Statements *

* Excerpts from *HOLY GROUND: The Guide To Faith And Ecology* (© ARC, 1997), including Declarations and Statements from Assisi 1986, and Windsor 1995

"Our forests, lands, waters and wildlife are still healthy and rich in biological diversity, because as Shamanists, we behold nature with awe and reverence, and hold all life, even landscapes, as sacred."

Dr. Manishev, Altai Republic
CoDoCa Conference, Urumqi, 1998

"We will know much if we can answer one question: will life in the next century be less stable than it is now?"

Eugene Linden
THE FUTURE IN PLAIN SIGHT:
Nine Clues To The Coming Instability, 1998

ཡོངས་སྐྱབས་མགོན་སྐུ་ཕྲེང་བཅུ་བཞི་པ་ཏཱ་ལའི་བླ་མ་བསྟན་འཛིན་རྒྱ་མཚོ་མཆོག་གི་གསུང་འཕྲིན།

The Rolex Awards for Enterprise

དཔར་བསྒྲུས་དབང་ཆ།

ནང་ཆོས་ཚོགས་ནས་རང་བྱུང་ཁམས་ལ་ལྟ་ཕྱོགས་ཀྱི་ལས་འགུལ།
ད ཀ ར ་ ཆ ག ས །

༤༥། ནང་ཆོས་ནས་རང་བྱུང་ཁམས་ཕྱོགས་བཅུ་རྩལ་ཞེས་པའི་དཔེ་དེབ་དང་། ལས་འགུལ་འདི་བཞིན་འགྲོ་བ་མིས་འདོད་ཚམ་གྱིས་རང་བཞིན་གྱི་ཁོར་ཡུག་སྲུང་སྐྱོབ་ཐོག་གཏོར་སྐྱོན་ཤུགས་ཆེར་ཡོང་བཞིན་པ་བཀག་འགོག་བྱེད་ཐབས་སུ་སྐྱོབ་གསོ་ཞིབ་པའི་ཡག་ཆེའི་ལས་འགུལ་གསར་པ་ཞིག་ཡིན།

ལོ་ཉིས་སྟོང་ཟ་བརྒྱའི་ཇོན་གྱི་ལམ་ལུགས་དང་། སྐྱོབ་གསོའི་ལམ་སྟོན་གསར་ཞིབ་བྱས་པར་གཅིག་བྱས་ན་ཡ་མཚན་མདོག་ཁ་པོ་རེད། ཚ་དོན་འདི་བཞིན་གལ་ཆེར་བརྟེན་གཞུང་དང་། སྒེར་གྱི་ཚོགས་ཁག་བཅས་ནས་འགན་འཁྱེར་གྱིས་རང་བྱུང་ཁམས་སྲུང་སྐྱོབ་གྱིས་ལས་འགུལ་བྱས་པ་ནས་མི་ལོ་བཅུ་ཕྲག་གཉིས་ཙམ་འགྲོ་གི་ཡོད་པ་མ་ཟད། དེང་གི་འཆར་ཡོངས་ཁྱབ་ཏུ་ཁས་ལེན་བྱེད་བཞིན་ཡོད། དེ་འདྲ་སོང་ཙང་དེང་དུས་ཀྱི་དཀའ་ངལ་གྱི་རྒྱུ་རྐྱེན་འདི་སེལ་ཐབས་སུ་ང་རང་ཚོའི་བསམ་བློའི་ནང་ཁ་རབས་ཀྱི་བསྒྲུབ་བྱ་རྣམས་ལག་བསྟར་གང་གི་ཕྱིར་བྱེད་ཀྱི་མེད་དམ། རྒྱུ་མཚན་ནི། ཁོར་ཡུག་སྲུང་སྐྱོབ་ཀྱི་ལས་འགུལ་ལས་དེར་གཏོར་སྐྱོན་གནོད་མཁན་ཆེས་རྒྱ་ཆེ་བ་ཡོད་པར་སོང་ཙང་ད་ལྟའི་ཁོར་ཡུག་སྲུང་སྐྱོབ་ཀྱི་ལས་འགུལ་གྱི་དཀའ་ངལ་སེལ་ཐབས་ཀྱི་མེད།

ཁོར་ཡུག་སྲུང་སྐྱོབ་ཀྱི་ལས་འགུལ་འདི་ཕལ་ཆེར་ཇེ་དྲག་གིས་དཀའ་ངལ་འཕྲད་པ་ལས་བྱུང་བ་ཞིག་ཡིན་གཤིས་དེ་ཡང་སྤྱིས་ལུགས་ཚན་རིག་ཐོག་གི་དཀའ་ངལ་ལ་དམིགས་ཏེ་འཚུགས་བཀྱུན་རྩ་ཚོགས་པའི་ལམ་ནས་ལས་འགུལ་ཞིབ་ཐབས་བྱ་རྒྱ་དེ་རེད། འོན་ཀྱང་ད་ཡོད་རང་བྱུང་ཁམས་དང་། རང་བྱུང་གཉེར་སོགས་ལ་གནོད་འཚབས་བྱས་པ་དང་། ད་ཆ་རྒྱ་ཆེར་བྱེད་བཞིན་པོར་ཁ་སལ་སྤྲོད་ཡང་དག་པར་བྱེད་ཐུབ་མེད།

དེའི་རྒྱུ་མཚན་གཅིག་ནི། སྲོག་ཆགས་དང་། རྩི་ཤིང་རྩ་ཚོགས་པར་གནོད་འཚབས་ཆེ་ཆེར་བྱེད་པ་ཤེས་བཞིན་དུ་དེ་ལས་སྐྱོབ་པའི་ཐབས་སུ་དཔལ་འབྱོར་སོགས་ཀྱི་དཀའ་ངལ་ལ་བརྟེན་ནས་ལས་འགུལ་འདི་བཞིན་འགོ་ཚུགས་ཐུབ་མེད། ཡང་རྒྱུ་མཚན་གཞན་ཞིག་ནི། དེར་དོ་སྣང་མ་བྱས་པར་དེ་སྔར་ལུས་རྗེས་ཛ་དྲག་ཤུགས་ཆེ་འགྲོ་ཀབས་འ་དུམ་མ་འདུས་པའི་སྐབས་སུ་སྤྱི་བུར་ལས་འགུལ་རྩམ་དགོས་པའི་རྐྱེན་གྱི་རེད།

རྒྱུ་མཚན་གསུམ་པ་ནི། ཟི་སྐར་སྲུང་སྐྱོབ་བྱེད་པའི་གནས་ལུགས་ཉམས་ལེན་བྱེད་པའི་ཚོགས་དང་། དེ་བཞིན་དཔལ་འབྱོར་དང་། ཡར་རྒྱས། ལྷ་མཐུད་སྟོན་ཕྱོགས་འདེབས་ལས། མདོར་ན་སྟོང་གསུམ་གྱི་སྟོང་ཆེན་པོ་འཛིག་རྟེན་ཁམས་གནས་པའི་སྲོག་རྩར་བརྟེན་ནན་ཏན་བརྗོད་པ་ཞིག་ཡིན།

གདམས་ངག་འདི་ནི་ད་ལྟ་དང་། མ་འོངས་པའི་མི་རབས་རྣམས་ཀྱི་བདེ་སྐྱིད་གལ་གནད་ཤིན་ཏུ་ཆེ་བའང་། དེ་ལ་སུས་ཀྱང་དོ་སྣང་བྱས་མེད། ནང་ཆོས་ཕྱོགས་ནས་རང་བྱུང་ཁམས་སྲུང་སྐྱོབ་ཀྱི་ལྟ་བ་འདི་ནི་རིག་གཞུང་འདྲ་མིན་དང་། རྒྱུ་ཚོགས་དང་། མི་རིགས་སོ་སོས་དཀའ་ངལ་དེ་ལས་ཐོག་ཐབས་ཀྱི་ཐུལ་པའི་ཐོག་ནན་ཏན་བརྗོད་ཀྱི་ཡོད།

མ་འོངས་པའི་དཔལ་འབྱོར་དང་། ཚན་རིག་གི་གནད་དོན་ཐོག་གལ་ཆེར་འགྱུར་ཡོད་སྟབས་རྣམ་པར་བྱང་ཆུབ་པའི་གཞུང་དང་། ཚོང་དོན་དབུ་གཙོ་རྣམ་པས་ལས་འགུལ་དེར་ཞུགས་དགོས་པའི་འབོད་བསྐུལ་བྱས་ནའང་། ཁོང་ཚོས་རྒྱ་མཚན་དེ་ཙམ་ལ་དགོངས་ནས་ལག་ལེན་བསྟར་མི་ཡོང་སྟབས། རང་བྱུང་ཁམས་གཏོར་བཤིགས་བྱེད་པ་དང་། དེ་སྲུང་སྐྱོབ་བྱེད་མཁན་ཚོས་རྒྱ་མཚན་སྣ་ཚོགས་ལ་རྟེན་ཏེ་བྱེད་ཀྱི་ཡོད་པ་མངོན་གསལ་དོད་པོ་རེད། ཡོངས་ལ་ཁྱབ་པའི་བླ་མ་མཆོག་ནས་དེའི་ཐོག་གསུང་འཕྲིན་བཀའ་སློབ་གནང་བ་ལྟར། འཛམ་གླིང་སྣོད་བཅུད་ལ་གཏོར་སྐྱོན་གཏོང་བ་དེ་ཡི་འགྲོ་བ་མིའི་འདོད་རྔམ་གྱི་རང་བཞིན་ལ་བརྟེན་ནས་བྱུང་བ་ཞིག་རེད། དེ་དང་དེ་བཞིན་གྱི་འགྲོ་བ་མིས་སེམས་ཅན་གཞན་ལ་གུས་བརྩི་མེད་པའི་རྐྱེན་གྱི་གོམས་གཤིས་དེ་ཉམས་བཟླག་འགྲོ་བ་ཡིན། ཞེས་བཀའ་སློབ་གནང་ཡོད།

རང་བྱུང་ཁམས་སྲུང་སྐྱོབ་བྱེད་མཁན་འགའ་ཤས་ཀྱིས་རང་ཉིད་དངོས་སུ་ནགས་གཞིབ་སོགས་གནས་དབེན་པའི་ཕྱོགས་སུ་བསྐྱོད་མ་ཐུབ་ནའང་། དེར་བསྐྱོད་ཐུབ་མཁན་གྱི་སྐུ་མཐུན་གཞན་ལ་རོགས་ཕན་བྱེད་ཀྱི་ཡོད། ཚོང་པ་སོགས་རང་ཉིད་ཀྱི་འཚོ་ལས་ཀྱི་ཁེ་ཕན་ལ་རྩིས་པ་དང་། དེ་བཞིན་ཕྱ་ཕྱུ་ཆོས་སེམས་ཅན་ལ་དགའ་སེམས་ཡོད་པའི་དབང་གི་ཁོང་ཚོའི་སེམས་ཅན་རྣམས་སྲུང་སྐྱོབ་བྱེད་དགོས་ཀྱི་ཡོད་ཅེས་ཐད་ཀར་བརྗོད་དེ་སྲུང་སྐྱོབ་བྱེད་ཀྱི་ཡོད།

ཚན་རིག་པ་འགའ་ཞིག་ལོ་ལོའི་སློབ་ཚན་ཐོག་ཚད་ལྡན་མཁས་པ་ཚོས་ལས་འགུལ་དེར་དོ་སྣང་བྱེད་དགོས་པ་ནི། སེམས་ཅན་རྣམས་ཀྱི་ལུགས་ཀྱི་འབྱུང་ཁུངས་སོགས་འདྲ་མིན་ལ་བརྟེན་ཏེ་བྱེད་ཀྱི་ཡོད། ངས་ཤེས་འཚོར་བྱུང་བའི་ནང་ཚན་རིག་པའི་ཁོངས་ནས་གཙན་གཟན་གྱི་རིགས་ལ་ཉམས་ཞིབ་པ་རྣམས་ཀྱི་ལས་དོན་དེར་མཁྱེན་ཡོན་རྩེ་ཕུད་ཅན་ཚོས་རང་བྱུང་ཁམས་སྲུང་སྐྱོབ་ཀྱི་ལས་འགུལ་བྱེད་ཀྱི་ཡོད།

ད་སྔའི་འཛམ་གླིང་འདི་བཞིན་ད་ཡོད་བཞིན་གནས་ཐབས་སུ་ཐུགས་རྒྱང་རིང་པོས་བཙོས་ཐབས་སྣ་ཚོགས་ཡོད་ཁོངས། ནང་པའི་ཆོས་ནས་གསུངས་པའི་བསླབ་ཚིག་རྣམས་དེ་ཁོངས་ཡོད། དེ་ལས་གལ་ཆེ་བ་དེའི་སྐོར་ཤེས་ཡོན་སློབ་གསོ་ཞིབ་ཐབས་དེ་ཡིན།

ནང་ཆོས་དང་། རང་བྱུང་ཁམས་ཀྱི་སྲུང་སྐྱོབ་ཅེས་པའི་ལས་འགུལ་འདི་ཁོངས་རྩོམ་དེབ་འདིའི་བཞིན་རང་བྱུང་ཁམས་སྲུང་སྐྱོབ་བྱེད་མཁན་གྱི་ནང་པའི་ས་ཁུལ་ཙམ་མ་ཡིན་པར་འཛམ་གླིང་ནང་རང་བྱུང་ཁམས་ལ་གཏོར་སྐྱོན་འགྲོ་བཞིན་པའི་ས་ཁུལ་ཚང་མར་གལ་ཆེར་འགྱུར་ཡོད།

དཔེ་རིབ་འདིའི་ནང་ཐ་ན་རང་ཉིད་ཀྱི་ཁྱིམ་ཚང་དང་། དེ་བཞིན་རྒྱ་ཆེར་སློབ་འཁྲིད་དང་། དབུ་འཁྲིད་ཚོས་ཀྱང་དེ་སྲུང་སྐྱོབ་བྱེད་དགོས་སྐོར་རང་བྱུང་ཁམས་སྲུང་སྐྱོབ་ཀྱི་སློབ་སྟོན་ཆ་ཚང་བཀོད་ཡོད། དཔེ་རིབ་འདི་བཞིན་པོ་ཁྲིམ་བྱེད་ཕྱོགས་སུ་རང་བྱུང་ཁམས་སྲུང་སྐྱོབ་བྱེད་དགོས་པ་གལ་ཆེ་ཡིན་ཚུལ་དང་། རིག་པ་གཞུང་། ཁས་ལེན་གྱི་བསམས་གཞིས། བརྙ་བརྗོད་མཁྱེན་རྟ་ངས་པོ་རིམ་བཞིན་ཆ་ཚང་དཔོད་ཡོད།

ཀྱ་ཞབས་མཁས་དབང་ཆན་ལུ་མན་ཀ་ཐིལ་ཤིང་གིས་རང་བྱུང་ཁམས་སྲུང་སྐྱོབ་སྐོར་ནང་ཆོས་ཀྱི་བསླབ་བྱ་དང་། མཁས་དབང་ཐེ་ཏན་གྱིས་ད་ལྟའི་ཁོར་ཡུག་གི་གནས་སྟངས་བཅས་མཁས་པའི་རྣམ་དཔྱོད་ཀྱི་གྲུ་ཚལ་ལས་འདྲངས་པའི་རྩོམ་རིགས་དེ་དག་གིས་དཔེ་རིབ་འདིའི་པོ་དོན་གསལ་པོ་རྟོགས་ཐུབ་ཀྱི་ཡོད། རང་བྱུང་ཁམས་སྲུང་སྐྱོབ་དེ་དུས་དང་རྣམ་པ་ཀུན་ཏུ་རང་ཉིད་ཀྱི་བསམས་སྤྱོད་དུ་འགྱུར་བ་ན། མི་ཚེའི་ཕྱུགས་ཚོད་ཀྱང་ལེགས་སུ་འགྲོ་བ་ཡིན། ནང་པའི་ཆོས་ནས་གསུངས་པའི་བདེ་སྐྱིད་དང་། ཁོར་ཡུག་སྲུང་སྐྱོབ་ཀྱི་ཆ་བ་ནི། དེང་དུས་ཁོར་ཡུག་འཛིན་སྐྱོང་སྲིད་བྱུས་ནང་མངོན་གསལ་དོད་དུ་འགྲོ་གི་ཡོད།

ནང་ཆོས་ནང་། རང་བྱུང་ཁམས་སྲུང་སྐྱོབ་ཀྱི་ལས་འགུལ་འདི་བཞིན་འགོ་ཚུགས་པ་ནས། དེ་དང་འབྲེལ་བ་ཡོད་པ་རེར་ངོས་རང་དགའ་ཐོབ་ཆེན་པོ་བསྐྱེད་བྱུང་། ཕྱི་ལོ་ ༡༩༧༩ ལོར་ལས་འགུལ་འགོ་བཙུགས་མཁན་ནན་ལི་ཝེཔ་འཛམ་གླིང་གཅན་གཟན་མ་དངུལ་བརྒྱ་ཚོགས་ཀྱི་སློབ་སྟོན་པ་བྱེད་བཞིན་པའི་སྐབས་རང་བྱུང་སྲུང་སྐྱོབ་པ་ཆོས་འཛམ་གླིང་ཚོས་ལུགས་ཁག་ནས་རོགས་མགོན་ཞུ་དགོས་ཀྱི་རེད་གསུངས། ཁོང་ནས་རྒྱ་ནག་དང་འབྲེལ་བ་བཟོ་ཐབས་ཀྱི་བསམ་ཚུལ་བརྟན་པ་ལྟར། རྒྱ་ནག་དང་འབྲེལ་བ་བཟོས་གནང་། ལས་འགུལ་དེའི་ཐོག་མ་མང་ཕྱུག་ལས་གནང་མཐར་ཁོང་ལ་ཨེ་སུ་ཟིན་ཞེས་མཚན་འདོགས། དེ་རྗེས་ཁོང་སོང་སྐོར་དུ་འཛམ་གླིང་གཅན་གཟན་དངུལ་གསོག་ཀྱི་ཁྲིམ་འཛུགས་ཤིག་ཀྱང་རོགས་མགོན་ཞུས་ཡོད།

མཐར་ཕྱི་ལོ་ ༡༩༨༥ ལོར་ཁོར་ཡུག་སྲུང་སྐྱོབ་ལས་འགུལ་འདི་བཞིན་འཚར་འགོད་བཞིན་དབུ་འཁྲིད་གནང་། ལོ་གཉིས་ནང་ལས་འགུལ་འདིས་ནང་ཆོས་ཀྱི་བསླབ་བྱ་ན ལ་རང་བྱུང་ཁམས་ལ་མིའི་འགན་དབང་ཇི་ཡོད་གསལ་པོ་སྟོན་ཐུབ་པ་བྱུང་ཡོད་པ་མ་ཟད། ཁོར་ཡུག་ཐོག་ཀུན་སྤྱོད་འཁྱེར་སྟངས་ཐོག་ལའང་མི་མང་གི་སེམས་འཁུར་ཆེ་རུ་སོང་ཡོད།

རྩ་བའི་ཁོར་ཡུག་སྲུང་སྐྱོབ་ཐོག་ཀུན་སྤྱོད་འཁྱེར་སྟངས་རང་ཉིད་ཀྱི་མི་ཚེ་དང་། ལས་ཀའི་ཐོག་ཕལ་ཆེ་པོས་ཞིག་ཆགས་ཡོད། དེར་བརྟེན་སྲོག་གི་ལྗོན་ཤིང་དང་། དེའི་དམིགས་ཡུལ་ནང་ཁོར་ཡུག་ཐོག་ཀུན་སྤྱོད་འཁྱེར་སྟངས་ཕྱུགས་ཆེ་ཕ་ལག་ཡོད་པར་ངོས་རང་དགའ་ཐོབ་ལེ་ནུག་བྱུང་།

གོང་ས་ཏཱ་ལའི་བླ་མ་མཆོག་ནང་པ་ཙམ་མ་ཡིན་པར་འཛམ་གླིང་ཡོངས་ཀྱིས་བརྩེ་ཞུ་བའི་ཆོས་ཉིད་ཀྱི་དབུ་འཁྲིད་ཡང་དག་པ་ཞིག་ཡིན། ཁོང་གིས་ལས་འགུལ་འདི་འགོ་ཚུགས་པ་ནས་ད་བར་བཀའ་སློབ་རྒྱབ་སྐྱོར་བཀའ་དྲིན་ཆེ་བ་བཞིན། ང་ཚོ་ཆོས་ལུགས་གཞན་གྱི་དབུ་འཁྲིད་རྣམས་ཀྱིས་ཀྱང་གོང་ས་ཏཱ་ལའི་བླ་མའི་སྲོག་གི་ལྗོན་ཤིང་དང་གསུངས་པའི་ཁོར་ཡུག་ཐོག་ཀུན་སྤྱོད་འཁྱེར་སྟངས་ཀྱི་གསུང་འབྲེལ་ལ་དཔེ་མཚོན་གནང་རོགས་ཞེས་རེ་བསྐུལ་ཞུ་གི་ཡོད།

རང་བྱུང་སྣོད་ཁམས་ལ་སྲུང་སྐྱོབ་དགོས་པའི་གསུང་འཕྲིན།

༄༅། །ང་ཚོས་ཤེས་གསལ་ལྟར། འགྲོ་བ་མིའི་ཁྱེད་ནོར་རྣམས་ལ་རྩི་སྲུང་མི་བྱེད་པའི་མིའི་བྱ་སྤྱོད་ཀྱིས་འཛམ་གླིང་ས་སྟེང་གི་ཞི་བདེ་དང་སྲོག་ཆགས་རྣམས་རྒྱུན་གནས་མི་ཐུབ་པའི་ཉེན་ཁ་བཟོས་ཡོད་པ་རེད།

རང་བྱུང་གི་བཀོད་པ་དང་། དེ་དག་གི་བདག་འབྲས་བཅུད་ནོར་རྣམས་ཀྱི་གཏོར་བཅོམ་ནི།། མི་ཤེས་པ་དང་། འདོད་ཧམས། སྲོག་ཆགས་ལ་རྩི་མཐོང་མེད་པ་བཅས་ལས་བྱུང་བ་ཞིག་རེད། རྩི་མཐོང་མེད་པའི་གཤིས་སྤྱོད་འདི་འགྲོ་བ་མིའི་མི་རབས་ཐོག་ཁྱབ་གདལ་དུ་འགྲོ་བཞིན་ཡོད་པས། གལ་ཏེ་འཛམ་གླིང་གི་ཞི་བདེ་ཞེས་པ་དེ་དངོས་བདེན་གྱི་གནས་ཚུལ་ཞིག་ཏུ་མ་གྱུར་པ་དང་། རང་བྱུང་ཁམས་ཀྱི་གཏོར་བཅོམ་ད་ཡོད་ཀྱི་གོམ་འགྲོས་དེ་འདི་མུར་གནས་ན། འབྱུང་འགྱུར་གྱི་མི་རབས་རྣམས་ནས་ཉམས་རྒུད་རྒྱ་ཆེར་སོང་ཟིན་པའི་གླིང་སྣོད་ཅིག་ལ་བརྒྱུད་འཛིན་བདག་དབང་བྱ་དགོས་སུ་གྱུར་ངེས་རེད། རང་རེའི་ཕ་མེས་རྣམས་ནས་འཛམ་གླིང་འདི་ནོར་བཅུད་ཀྱིས་ཕྱུག་ཅིང་། དགོས་འདོད་འཛད་མེད་འཛོ་བ་ཞིག་ཏུ་མྱོང་གནང་བྱུང་ཡོད་པ་དེ་ལྟར་རེད།

འདས་པའི་དུས་སུ་སྐྱེ་བོ་མང་པོ་ཞིག་ནས་རང་བྱུང་ཁམས་ཀྱི་དངོས་པོ་རྣམས་ལ་ཧྲི་ཙམ་ལོངས་སྤྱོད་ཀྱང་། འཛད་མཐའ་མེད་པའི་རང་བཞིན་ཞིག་ཏུ་གནས་པ་མཐོང་གི་ཡོད་ཀྱང་། ད་ཆ་རང་བྱུང་ཁམས་ལ་བདག་སྤྱོད་གཅེས་སྐྱོང་ལེགས་པོ་ཞིག་མ་བྱས་ན་དེ་ལྟར་གནས་མི་ཐུབ་པ་ང་ཚོས་ཤེས་གསལ་རེད།

མི་ཤེས་པའི་དབང་ལས་འདས་པའི་དུས་སུ་གཏོར་བཅོམ་བྱུང་ཟིན་པ་རྣམས་ལ་བཟོད་བསྲན་བྱ་རྒྱུ་ཁག་པོ་མིན་ཀྱང་ད་ཆ་ང་ཚོས་གནས་ཚུལ་མང་པོ་ཞིག་ཤེས་རྟོ་ར་ཐུབ་ཀྱི་ཡོད་པར་བརྟེན། ཡ་རབས་མཛངས་སྤྱོད་ལ་བརྒྱུད་འཛིན་བདག་སྐྱོང་ཡོད་མེད་དང་། རང་ཐོག་ལ་འགན་འཁྲི་གང་ཞིག་བབ་ཡོད་མེད། མི་རབས་རྗེས་མར་གང་འདྲ་ཞིག་བརྒྱུད་སྐྱོང་དགོས་མིན་བཅས་ལ་ང་ཚོས་སླར་ཡང་བསམ་ཞིབ་བྱ་རྒྱུ་གལ་ཆེན་པོ་རེད། ད་ལྟའི་མི་རབས་འདི་འགྱུར་འགྲོས་ཀྱིས་མཚམས་ཤིག་ཡིན་པ་གསལ་པོ་རེད། འཛམ་གླིང་ཡོངས་སུ་ཕན་ཚུན་གོ་རྟོགས་སྤྲེལ་རེས་བྱེད་ཐུབ་ཀྱི་ཡོད་ཀྱང་། ཞི་བདེའི་ཆེད་དོན་ལྡན་གྱི་བགྲོ་གླེང་ལས་ཁ་གཏད་གདོང་གཏུགས་ཀྱི་ལངས་ཕྱོགས་དེ་མང་བ་ཡོང་བཞིན་པ་རེད།

འཛམ་གླིང་གི་ཆ་ཁ་ཤས་སུ་མིའི་རིགས་ལྟོགས་ཤི་ཐེབས་པ་དང་། སྲོག་ཆགས་གཞན་གྱི་རིགས་རྒྱ་སྟོངས་སུ་འགྲོ་བ་བཅས་ཀྱིས་མཚོན། དེང་དུས་ཀྱི་རྐྱེན་ངན་མང་པོ་འདི་དག་གིས་རྨད་དུ་བྱུང་བའི་ཚན་རིག་དང་འཕྲུལ་རིག་གི་དགེ་མཚན་བཟང་པོ་རྣམས་གལ་ཏེ་ཟིལ་གྱིས་མནན་མེད་ནའང་། དེ་མཉམ་འགྲན་བཟོད་པ་ལྟ་བུར་གྱུར་ཡོད། ཕྱིའི་མཁའ་དབྱིངས་ལ་ཉམས་ཞིབ་མང་པོ་བྱེད་བཞིན་པ་དང་དུས······མཚུངས། ས་སྟེང་གི་རྒྱ་མཚོ་རྣམས་དང་། མཚོ་ཆེན་ཁག །ཆུ་གཙང་ཡོད་པའི་ས་ཁུལ་རྣམས་དུག་རྫས་ངན་པའི་རླབས་ཀྱིས་ཆེས་ཆེར་བསླད་ཅིང་། དེ་དག་ཏུ་གནས་འཆའ་བའི་སྲོག་ཆགས་རྣམས་ཀྱི་ཐད་ལ་ད་དུང་མི་ཤེས་པ་དང་གོ་ལོག་རྒྱ་ཆེར་བྱེད་བཞིན་ཡོད་པ་རེད།

གླིང་འདིའི་སེམས་ཅན་གྱི་གནས་དང་། སེམས་ཅན་རྣམས་དང་། རྩེ་ཤིང་རི་
དང་། འབུ་སྲིན་རིགས་དང་། ཐ་ན་ཤིན་ཏུ་ཆེས་ཕྲ་བའི་སྲོག་ཆགས་རིགས་
ད་ཆ་ང་ཚོས་དཀོན་པོར་ཤེས་པ་རྣམས་འབྱུང་འགྱུར་མི་རབས་རྣམས་ཀྱིས་གཏན་
ནས་མི་ཤེས་པར་འགྱུར་ཉེན་ཡོད། དེའི་ཐད་ང་རང་ཚོར་ནུས་པ་དང་འགན་
ཡོད། ང་རང་ཚོས་ཁྱིམ་མ་དྲགས་གོང་ནས་ལག་ལེན་གྱི་བྱ་བ་ངེས་པར་བརྩམ་
དགོས་པ་རེད།། །།

ཏཱ་ལའི་བླ་མས་ ༡༩༨༦ ཕྱི་ཟླ་༦ ཚེས་༥ ལ།

དབྱིན་ཡིག་ནས་ཕབ་སྒྱུར་ཞུས།

༄༅། རང་བྱུང་ཁམས་སྲུང་སྐྱོབ་སྐོར་ནང་ཆོས་ཀྱི་བསླབ་བྱ།

ཆད་ལུ་མན་ཀ་ཕྱིལ་ལིང་།

ཕ་ཡི་ཡུམ་ལྷ་ཁང་ནི་ཐེང་ཁོག་གྲོང་འཁྱེར་ཉེ་འགྲམ་དུ་ཡོད་པའི་ནང་པའི་ལྷ་ཁང་ཞིག་རེད། ལྷ་ཁང་འདི་འགྲུལ་པ་མང་པོ་ཞིག་ལ་དགའ་བསུ་ཞུ་གི་ཡོད་པ་རེད། འགྲུལ་པ་དེ་རྣམས་བྱ་ཁྲུང་ཁྲུང་དཀར་མོའི་རིགས་ཤིག་རེད། བྱ་དེ་དག་སྟོན་ཁ་དང་དགུན་ཁ་ལྷ་ཁང་དེར་སྡོད་སྐབས་ལྷ་ཁང་དེ་དང་། ཤིང་སྡོང་ཚང་མ་བྱ་སྐྱུག་གིས་དཀར་པོ་བཟོ་གི་ཡོད་པ་རེད། ཡིན་ནའང་ལྷ་ཁང་དེའི་དགེ་འདུན་པ་རྣམས་ཀྱི་དེར་ཐུགས་བསུན་མ་གནང་བ་དང་། བྱ་ལ་དགའ་བའི་སྐྱེ་བོ་རྣམས་ཀྱིས་དགའ་བསུའི་རང་བཞིན་དུ་འཆར་གྱི་ཡོད་པ་རེད། ཁྲུང་ཁྲུང་དཀར་མོའི་རིགས་འདི་བཞིན་ལྷ་ཁང་དེའི་ནང་གཞིས་ཆགས་རྒྱུ་བྱུང་ཐུབ་པ་དེས་མ་གནོགས་ཐ་ཡི་ལེན་ཊེར་བྱ་རིགས་འདི་བཞིན་རྩ་སྟོང་འགྲོ་རྒྱུའི་ཉེན་ཁ་ཡོད་པ་རེད།

འཁོར་•••ཡུག་དང་སྲོག་ཆགས་ཐོག་མཁྱེན་ལྡན་རྣམས་ཀྱི་བཞེད་ཚུལ་ལ་བྱ་རིགས་འདི་བཞིན་སྲུང་སྐྱོབ་བྱེད་རྒྱུ་ནི་གལ་ཆེན་པོ་ཡིན་པ་རེད། གང་ལགས་ཟེར་ན་བྱ་འདིའི་ཟས་གཙོ་བོ་དེ་འབྲས་ཟ་མཁན་གྱི་སྦུག་པའི་འབུ་རིགས་ཞིག་ཡིན་པ་རེད། གལ་ཏེ་བྱ་དེ་མེད་པ་ཡིན་ན། འབུ་འདིའི་གྲངས་འཕེལ་རྒྱས་སུ་ཕྱིན་ནས་དེ་འགོག་ཐབས་སུ་འབུ་སྨན་བེད་སྤྱོད་བྱ་དགོས་བྱུང་ན་དེ་དུག་གི་ལས་ཀའི་འཁོར་ཡོ་གསར་པ་ཞིག་འགོ་འཛུགས་རྒྱུ་ཡིན་པ་དེ་བརྗོད་མ་དགོས་པ་རེད།

ཁྲུང་ཁྲུང་གི་རིགས་འདི་སྐྱབ་པའི་ངོ་བོ་གང་ཙམ་ནང་ཆོས་ཀྱི་བསླབ་བྱའི་ཐོག་ནས་སྤྱི་དང་གསེར་གྱི་བྱ་སྤྱོད་ལ་བརྟེན་ནས་ཁྲུང་ཁྲུང་གི་རིགས་བསླབ་བྱས་འདི་བཞིན་སྲུང་སྐྱབ་བྱས་པའི་དངོས་དཔང་སྒྲུབ་འབྲས་གསལ་པོ་ཞིག་རེད། ཉེ་བའི་ལོ་བཅུ་ཕྲག་འགའ་ཤས་རིང་ཟ་ཡེ་རྒྱལ་ཁབ་ཀྱི་རང་བྱུང་ཁམས་ལ་གནོད་འཚེ་ཤུགས་ཆེར་བྱུང་ཡོད་པ་རེད། ལོ་ངོ་ལྔ་བཅུ་སྔོན་དུ་རྒྱལ་ཁབ་ཀྱི་ས་ཁྱོན་བརྒྱ་ཆ་ ༨༠ ཙམ་ནགས་ཚལ་གྱིས་ཁེངས་ནས་ཡོད་པ་ད་ཆ་བརྒྱ་ཆ་ ༡༡ ལས་མེད་པ་རེད། བྱ་བྱིའུ་དང་། རི་དྭགས་གཅན་གཟན། རྩི་ཤིང་རྩ་ཚོགས་པ་མང་པོ་ཞིག་རྩ་སྟོང་འགྲོ་རྒྱུའི་ཉེན་ཁ་ཡོད་པ་མ་ཟད། རིགས་འགའ་ཤས་རྩ་མེད་དུ་ཕྱིན་ཟིན་པ་རེད།

ཟ་ཡེ་ནང་རང་བྱུང་ཁམས་དང་རང་བྱུང་རྫས་ལ་ཉམས་ཆགས་ཆེན་པོ་ཕྱིན་ཡོད་པའི་རྐྱེན་གྱི་དེང་སང་གྲོང་གསེབ་ཁག་མང་པོའི་ནང་འཚོ་བའི་གནས་སྟངས་ཞན་པས་ཡུལ་མི་ཚོར་དཀའ་ངལ་མང་པོ་ཞིག་འཕྲད་ཀྱི་ཡོད་པ་རེད། རྒྱལ་ས་ཟིང་ཀོག་ལ་ཆུ་སྐྱུག་ཡང་སེ་ཡོང་གི་དཀའ་ངལ་དང་། ཡང་རྒྱལ་ཁབ་ཀྱི་བྱང་ཤར་ས་ཁུལ་ལ་ཆར་པ་དུས་ཐོག་མ་བབས་པའི་དཀའ་ངལ་སོགས་མཚོར་ན་ཡུལ་མི་ཚོར་འཚོ་བ་བསྐྱལ་རྒྱུར་དཀའ་ངལ་ཁ་ཙང་ཡོད་པ་རེད།

ཟ་ཡེ་ལེན་ཀ་ཡུལ་གྱི་རང་བྱུང་སྡོད་ལ་གཏོར་སྐྱོན་ཤུགས་ཆེར་བྱུང་ཡོད་པ་རེད་ལ་དེང་སང་འཛམ་གླིང་ནང་རང་བྱུང་ཁམས་དང་། སྡོད་ལ་སྲུང་བརྩི་མེད་པའི་འདོད་རྫས་ཀྱིས་བེད་སྤྱོད་བྱེད་སྟངས་དེ་ལ་བརྟས་ཚོད་དུ་རང་བྱུང་ཁམས་དང་སྡོད་ཀྱི་རིགས་རྩ་མེད་འགྲོགས་མྱུར་འགྲོ་གྲིད་པ་རེད། དེ་འདྲར་བརྟེན་བྱ་ཁྲུང་ཁྲུང་གི་རིགས་དེ་དང་འདྲ་བའི་རང་བྱུང་ཁམས་དང་སྡོད་ཀྱི་རིགས་མང་པོ་ཞིག་སེམས་ཅན་ཐམས་ཅད་ལ་ཕན་པའི་བསམ་བློ་གཏོང་དགོས་པའི་བསླབ་བྱ་དེའི་འབྲས་བུ་ཞིག་ཡིན་པ་རེད། ཡིན་འང་རང་བྱུང་ཁམས་དང་། སྡོད་ཀྱི་གཏོར་གཞིགས་གཏོང་མཁན་གྱི་པོ་འདོད་རྫས་ཅན་དང་། དོ་སྣང་མེད་མཁན་དེ་ཚོས་ཕོ་རེད་ཚོ་ཡིན་པའི་ཡིད་ཆེས་ཡོད་རེད། ནང་པ་ཅིས་བརྗོད་ཀྱི་མེད། ཇི་ལྟར་རང་བྱུང་ཁམས་དང་སྡོད་ཀྱི་ཐོག་ཆོས་ལུགས་འདྲ་མིན་དབར་ལྟ་སྤྱོད་འཕྲེར་ཕྱོགས་མི་འདྲ་བ་ཡོད་པ་བཞིན། དེའི་ཕོ་དོན་ལེན་ཕྱོགས་ཀྱང་མི་དང་། མིའི་དབར་ཁྱད་པར་ཆེན་པོ་ཡོད་པ་རེད། ཆོས་ལུགས་ཚང་མའི་ནང་མིའི་རྣམ་དཔྱོད་འདྲ་མིན་སྣ་ཚོགས་པ་བཞིན་འཛམ་གླིང་འདིའི་ནང་ནང་པ་མི་གྲངས་ས་ཡ་གསུམ་བརྒྱ་ནས་དྲུག་བརྒྱ་བར་ཡོད་པའི་ནང་ཁྱད་པར་འཕགས་པའི་སྐྱེས་བུ་དམ་པ་དང་། མིང་ཙམ་གྱི་ནང་པ་ཡིན་པ་སོགས་སྤྱིར་ ཚོགས་ཡོད་པ་རེད།

ནང་པ་སངས་རྒྱས་ཀྱི་ཆོས་ལུགས་ནི་གསེར་གྱི་ལྟ་སྤྱོད་ལ་གལ་ཆེར་འཛིན་ཏེ་ལྟ་བ་དང་སྤྱོད་པ་གཉིས་ཐོག་ཞིབ་འཇུག་གི་ལམ་མ་ནོར་བར་ཉམས་ལེན་གྱི་ཐར་པ་ཐོབ་དགོས་པ་ཞིག་ཡིན་པ་རེད།

འཛམ་གླིང་གི་ཆོས་ལུགས་ཆེ་བ་གཞན་གྱི་ནང་དེ་འདྲ་བའི་བསླབ་བྱ་དང་། ངོས་འཛིན་བྱེད་སྲོལ་མེད་པ་དེས་ནང་པའི་ཆོས་ཀྱི་བསླབ་བྱ་ཐུང་མ་ཡིན་པ་ཞིག་ལ་ངོས་འཛིན་བྱེད་ཀྱི་ཡོད་པ་རེད།

རང་བྱུང་ཁམས་ཀྱི་ཚན་རིག་པས་རང་བྱུང་ཁམས་སྲུང་སྐྱོབ་དགོས་པའི་སློབ་གསོ་དང་། རྒྱུ་མཚན་མང་པོ་ཞིག་ནང་པ་སཀྱས་པའི་ཆོས་ཀྱི་བསླབ་བྱའི་ནང་ནས་ཐོབ་ཀྱི་ཡོད་པ་རེད།

ནང་ཆོས་ནང་རང་བྱུང་ཁམས་དབང་དུ་འགྱུར་བ་ལས་མཉམ་དུ་གནས་ཐུབ་པ་དེ་གལ་ཆེ་ཡིན་པ་བསླབས་ཡོད་པ་རེད། ནང་ཆོས་གཉིང་ཟབ་ཉམས་ལེན་གནང་མཁན་རྣམས་ཀྱི་ངོ་ ཚོ་ཁྲེལ་མེད་ཀྱི་གནོད་འཚེའི་བྱ་སྤྱོད་ལ་རྒྱང་བར་བྱེད་པ་ལས་རང་བྱུང་ཁམས་སྲུང་སྐྱོབ་ཡོང་རྒྱུར་སྐུལ་ཞེན་གནང་གི་ཡོད་པ་རེད།

ནང་ཆོས་ཀྱི་སྙིང་དོན་ནི་སྙིང་རྗེ་ཡིན་པ་རེད། དེ་བཞིན་འཛམ་གླིང་འདིའི་ཐང་གི་འགྲོ་བ་མི་དང་སྲོག་ཆགས་གཞན་རྣམས་ལ་བརྩེ་མཐོང་ནང་བཟོད་སེམས་ཀྱི་མཉམ་དུ་གནས་དགོས་པའི་སྣུགས་གཏོན་རྟོན་གྱི་ཡོད་པ་རེད། ང་ཚོས་བརྟག་ཞིབ་བྱས་པའི་སྙིང་པོར་ནང་ཆོས་ཉམས་ལེན་བྱེད་མཁན་གྱི་ཡུལ་མང་པོའི་ནང་རང་བྱུང་ཁམས་ལ་སྲུང་སྐྱོབ་བྱེད་རྒྱུར་ཕན་ཡོན་ཆེན་པོ་བྱུང་ཡོད་པ་རེད། དཔེར་ན། ལང་ཀའི་ཡུལ་གྱི་རི་དྭགས་མང་ཆེ་བ་ཐར་རྒྱུན་བཞིན་གནས་ཐུབ་ཡོད་པ་དེ་ནི་ཡུལ་མི་རྣམས་དད་ལྡན་ནང་པ་ཡིན་པའི་རྐྱེན་གྱི་རེད། ཅེས་ཉམས་ཞིབ་བྱེད་མཁན་ཚོས་བཤད་ཀྱི་ཡོད།

རང་བྱུང་ཁམས་སྲུང་སྐྱོབ་བྱེད་རྒྱུ་དེ་ནི་གཞུང་འབྲེལ་གྱི་ལས་འགུལ་འགོ་འཛུགས་བྱས་པ་ཞིག་ཡིན། དེ་ནི་ཡུལ་དེའི་མི་མང་ནས་ཁས་ལེན་དང་། འདོད་སྤྲོར་མེད་ཚེ་གྲུབ་འབྲས་ཐོན་རྒྱུར་ཕན་ནུས་དེ་ཙམ་མེད་པ་རེད། རང་བྱུང་ཁམས་རྒྱུན་གནས་ཐུབ་པའི་ལས་འགུལ་གྱི་གྲུབ་འབྲས་ལེགས་པོ་བྱུང་བ་དེ་དག་གཙོ་བོ་ནང་དོན་རིག་པའི་བསམ་བློ་འཁྲིར་ཕྱོགས་ལ་རག་ལུས་ཡོད་པ་རེད།

ང་ཚོའི་བོད་རིགས་ཉམས་ཞིབ་འགན་འཛིན་རྣམས་ཀྱིས་ཉེ་བའི་འཚར་ལོ་རྒྱས་དྭན་ཐོག་ལ་བོད་ནང་རྐྱ་བ་དང་། གཡག འབྲོང་། ཤ་བ། དེ་བཞིན་བྱ་རིགས་ཀྱི་ཁྱུ་ལ་སོགས་པ་མང་པོ་ཞིག་མིའི་རྫོང་གནས་འབྲུག་ས་ཧོ་བུར་འཇིགས་སྐྲག་མེད་པའི་ངང་ཡོང་ནས་མཉམ་དུ་བརྫོད་པ་སོ་སོར་ཡོང་གི་ཡོད་པ་རེད། དེ་ནི་བོད་དེ་བཞིན་ནང་པའི་རྒྱལ་ཁབ་གཅིག་ཡིན་པའི་རྒྱུ་མཚན་ལ་བརྟེན་ནས་བྱུང་བ་ཞིག་རེད།

སྔོ་ཕམ་པའི་གནས་ཚུལ་ཞིག་ལ་གནས.ཧ་ངས་དེ་འགྱུར་བ་ཕྱིན་ནས་ད་ཆ་བོད་ནི་རང་བྱུང་ཁམས་དང་སྲོག་ཆགས་སོགས་ལ་རྟོད་འཚེ་ཐེ་མང་བྱུང་བའི་ཡུལ་ཞིག་ཏུ་བརྩིས་ཀྱི་ཡོད་པ་རེད།

འཛམ་གླིང་མཉམ་སྤྱིལ་རྒྱལ་ཚོགས་ཀྱི་འགྲོ་བ་མིའི་ཐོབ་འཐང་གི་ཚོགས་ཆུང་ལ་ཕུལ་བའི་དམིགས་བསལ་ལས་བཙོམས་དེའི་ནང་། བོད་ཀྱི་རྩི་ཤིང་ནགས་ཚལ་གྱིས་ཁྱབ་པའི་ས་ཁ་རྒྱ་ཚེ་རྩ་མེད་བཙོས་པ་དང་ཟར་རི་དྭགས་མང་པོ་གནས་པ་དེ་དག་ད་ཆ་རྩ་མེད་དུ་བཏང་ཡོད་པ་རེད་ཅེས་བཀོད་ཡོད་པ་རེད།

སངས་རྒྱས་ཀྱི་བསྟན་པའི་ལོ་རྒྱུས་ནང་ནང་ཤེས་ཀྱིས་རང་བྱུང་ཁམས་སྲུང་སྐྱོབ་ཐོག་ཕན་ཆེན་པོ་བྱུས་ཡོད་པ་རེད། ཞི་བའི་འཚར་ནང་པའི་འགོ་འཁྲིད་ཚོས་གནས་དོན་འདིའི་ཐོག་ནང་ཆོས་ལས་བཤད་པའི་ནང་དོན་རིག་པའི་བསླབ་བྱ་རྣམས་རང་བྱུང་ཁམས་སྲུང་སྐྱོབ་དང་ཟར་ཡོད་རྒྱུན་གནས་ཡོང་ཐབས་སུ་ཕན་ཐོགས་དང་། ཞབས་འདེགས་ཞུ་ཐུབ་ཀྱི་ཡོད་པའི་གསུང་གླེང་གནང་གི་ཡོད་པ་རེད།

༼ཁོང་ས་ ༼སྐྱབས་མགོན་ཏཱ་ལའི་བླ་མ་མཆོག་ནས་གསར་འགོད་པར་བཀའ་བཅལ་གསལ། དེང་སང་ཟར་ལས་ཉུག་པར་ང་ཚོས་རྒྱལ་སྤྱིའི་ལས་འགན་ཐོག་སེམས་འཁུར་བྱེད་དགོས་པ་ཞིག་ཡིན་ལ། དེ་ཡང་རྒྱལ་ཁབ་ཕན་ཚུན་དང་། མི་དང་མིའི་བར་དུ་མ་ཟད། མི་དང་སྲོག་ཆགས་གཞན་གྱི་རིགས་ལའང་སེམས་འཁུར་བྱེད་དགོས་པ་ཡིན།

སྤྱི་ཚོགས་ཀྱི་གནས་སྟངས་ཉམས་ཞིབ་པ་དང་རྩོམ་པ་པོ་སུ་ལག སི་བ་རག་སས་གསུངས་གསལ་འཛམ་གླིང་འདི་བཞིན་རྟོགས་འཛིངས་གང་འདྲ་ཞིག་ཏུ་འགྱུར་བ་ཡིན་ནའང་། ནང་ཆོས་ཀྱི་བསླབ་བྱ་དེ་དག་ཁ་ཡོད་ལག་ཡོད་ཕན་ནུས་ཡོད་པ་དང་སྤྱི་ཚོགས་ཀྱི་ཡར་རྒྱས་དང་། མཐུན་བསྒྲིལ་ཡོང་རྒྱུར་ཕན་ནུས་ཐུབ་པའི་གལ་ཆེའི་གཞི་རྩ་ཞིག་ཆགས་ཡོད་པ་རེད། ཀུ་ཞབས་སུ་ལག སི་བ་རག་ས་ཁོ་རང་ལ་གླིང་ཆེན་ཤེ་ཤ་ཡ་དང་འཛམ་གླིང་འཕོ་འགྱུར་འགྲོ་བའི་ནང་ཐ་ཡེ་ནང་པའི་ཆོས་ཀྱི་སྐད་འབོད་ཅེས་དང་། ཆེད་བརྗོད་ཀྱི་མིང་འབོད་བྱེད་ཀྱི་ཡོད་པ་རེད།

ཁོང་རང་རང་བྱུང་ཁམས་ལ་གཏོར་སྐྱོན་ཡོང་གི་ཡོད་པར་བརྟེན་ཁོང་རང་གིས་ནང་ཆོས་ཐོག་ནས་དེ་དག་སྲུང་སྐྱོབ་བྱེད་ཐུབ་པའི་ཡིད་མཆེས་ཀྱིས་ཐོག་ནང་ཆོས་ཀྱིས་རང་བྱུང་ཁམས་སྲུང་སྐྱོབ་བྱེད་དགོས་པའི་རྩོམ་བྲིས་དང་སྙན་དུ་པར་དང་གྲོ་སྡུད་ཀྲུབ་ཐག་ཐོག་གསུང་བཤད་གནང་བ་སོགས་ཀྱི་སྐུལ་རྟེན་གནང་གི་ཡོད་པ་རེད།

ད་དུང་མི་རྣམས་ཀྱི་ངོ་གལ་ཆེ་ཆུང་ལ་མ་ལྟོས་པར་རང་བྱུང་ཁམས་ལ་གནོད་འཚེ་བྱེད་བཞིན་པ་དེའི་ཐོག་ནང་ཆོས་ཀྱིས་དེར་ངོ་རྒོལ་བྱེད་ཀྱི་ཡོད་པ་རེད། ངོ་རྒོལ་དེ་ད་རྒྱ་ཆུང་ཆུང་ཞིག་ཡིན་ནའང་། ཞི་བའི་ཐོག་ནས་ལས་འགུལ་བྱས་པ་འདི་མེད་པ་ཀས་དགོས་པ་ཞིག་ཡིན་པ་དང་།

གལ་ཏེ་བསླབ་བྱ་དེ་དག་གལ་ཆེར་ཅིས་ནས་ལག་ལེན་དུ་བཀལ་ན་རང་བྱུང་ཁམས་ཟེར་ཡོད་རྒྱུན་གནས་ཐུབ་ཐབས་ལ་ལས་འགུལ་དེ་བཞིན་ང་ཚོའི་ལུང་པའི་ནང་ཤུགས་ཆེ་རུ་འགྲོ་རྒྱུ་རེད་ཅེས་གསུངས་ཡོད་པ་རེད།

ཉི་ཧོང་སྲིད་འཛིན་ཡ་སུ་ཧི་རོ་ ན་ཀ་སོ་ནེ་མཆོག་ནས་ཕྱི་ལོ་ ༡༩༨༥ ལོར་མཉམ་འབྲེལ་རྒྱལ་ཚོགས་ཀྱི་ལོ་བཞི་བཅུ་བསྐྱེས་པའི་དུས་དྲན་མཛད་རིམ་བཅས་ནས་འཛམ་གླིང་འདིའི་རང་བཞིན་འཛོམས་ཏུག་དང་། རིག་འདྲ་ཤིན་ཏུ་ཚོགས་ཡོད་པ་མུ་མཐུད་གནས་ཐུབ་ཐབས་ཀྱི་འབོད་བསྐུལ་ཞུས་གནང་ཡོད་པ་རེད།

སྔར་ཡང་ནང་ཆོས་ཀྱི་ཐོག་ནས་གསུང་བཤད་གནང་བ་དེའི་འབོད་བསྐུལ་དུ་འཛམ་གླིང་གི་ཀུན་སྤྱོད་གསར་པ་དགོས་རྒྱུ་ཞེས་པ་དེ་ནི་དུས་རབས་ཉི་ཤུ་པ་འདི་བཞིན་མི་རིགས་ཕན་ཚུན་ལ་བརྩི་བཀུར་དང་། མཉམ་གནས་ཐུབ་པ་དང་། མི་དང་རང་བྱུང་ཁམས་དབར་འབྲེལ་འཚམས་ཆ་སྙོམས་ཡོང་བའི་དུས་ཀབས་ཞེས་བརྗོད་ཐུབ་པ་བྱེད་རྒྱུ་དེ་ཡིན།

ཆོས་ཟབ་མོའི་དུས་ཀྱི་ནང་ཆོས་ཀྱི་བསླབ་བྱ་རྣམས་དུས་དེང་སང་གི་དགོས་དོན་ཐོག་ཕན་ཐོགས་ཡོད་པར་ངེས་འཛིན་བྱེད་མཁན་ཇི་མང་འགྲོ་བཞིན་པ་རེད།

ཐ་ཡེ་མཁས་པ་ཕོ་ཡ་ཏ་སི་གསུངས་གསལ་ལ་དེའི་རྒྱུ་མཚན་གཅིག་ནི། སྟོན་པ་བཅོམ་ལྡན་འདས་ཁོང་གི་བཀའ་དང་གསུངས་ཆོས་རྣམས་ཤེས་བྱ་ཙམ་དུ་མ་ཡིན་པར་དོན་དངོས་ལག་ལེན་དུ་འཁེལ་དགོས་པ་དེ་གལ་ཆེ་ཡིན་གསུང་པ་དེ་རེད་ཅེས་བརྗོད་ཡོད།

དབྱིན་ཇིའི་ཙམ་པ་ཕོ་ཤེཆ་ཇི་ཞབས་སི་ ནས་ནང་ཆོས་ཐོག་སློབ་སྦྱོང་གནང་ནས་མཐར་མ་གསུངས་གསལ། སྟོན་པའི་གསུངས་རྣམས་གསལ་པོ་དང་། དེང་དུས་ཀྱི་རིག་པ་དང་། བསམ་བློ་གཏོང་སྟངས་སོགས་དང་མཐུན་པོ་ཡོད་པ་དང་། འཛམ་གླིང་འདིའི་ནང་ནང་དོན་རིག་པ་གཏིང་ཟབ་པོས་ཡིན་པར་ངེས་འཛིན་བྱས་པར་རྩོད་པ་མེད་པ་ཞིག་རེད།

དཔེར་ན། ནང་ཆོས་ཀྱི་ཐོག་ནས་རང་བྱུང་ཁམས་ལ་བ་རྩ་ངས་ཀྱི་ལས་འགུལ་དང་། འདུ་བ་ཤེས་ཡོན་གྱི་ལས་རིགས་གཞན་ལ་ནང་ཆོས་ཀྱི་དམིགས་བསལ་ཤེས་བྱ་གསར་པའི་རིགས་སྤྲད་ཐུབ་ཀྱི་ཡོད་པ་རེད། མ་རིགས་པ་ཤེས་རབ་ཀྱི་གསལ་ཡག་ཡིན་ཙན་ནང་ཆོས་ཉམས་ལེན་བྱེད་མཁན་ཀྱི་ཕོ་

སུ་འདྲ་ཞིག་ཡིན་རུང་མ་རིགས་པ་དོར་ཏེ་ཤེས་རབ་དང་ཤེས་བྱ་ཇོན་དགོས་པ་ཞིག་རེད། དེ་བཞིན་དགེ་བའི་བཤེས་གཉེན་ལ་བརྩིགས་བཀུར་དང་། ནང་པའི་སློབ་དཔོན་ཁྱད་པར་དུ་འཕགས་པ་རྣམས་ལ་བསྙེན་བཀུར་བྱེད་དགོས་པ་ཡིན། དགེ་རྒན་ཚོས་རང་གི་སློབ་མ་རྣམས་རང་བྱུང་ཁམས་སྲུང་སྐྱོབ་ལས་འགུལ་ཉམས་ལེན་ཡོང་བའི་སློབ་གསོ་གནང་རྒྱུའི་མཐུན་རྐྱེན་ཆེད་དུ་ཡིག་ཆ་སོགས་པའི་ལག་ཆ་དགོས་ཀྱི་རེད། ང་ཚོའི་ལས་འགུལ་ཉམས་ཞིབ་པ་རྣམས་ནས་ལོ་ངོ་ ༢༥༠༠ སྔག་ཙམ་གོང་གི་རྒྱ་ཆེ་ལ་གཏིང་ཟབ་པའི་ནང་ཆོས་ཀྱི་གསུང་རབ་རྣམས་ཀྱང་རིགས་འདྲ་མིན་ནང་ཡོད་པ་བཅས་ལ་ཉམས་ཞིབ་གནང་སྟེ་མཐུན་རྐྱེན་སྤྲོད་ཐུབ་དགོས་པའི་ལས་འགན་ཡོད་པ་རེད། ཐོན་འགྲོའི་ཉམས་ཞིབ་ལས་འགུལ་བྱས་རྗེས་ཡིག་ཆ་རྣམས་ཁག་གཅིག་ཏུ་བསྡུ་རྒྱུ་རེད། དེའང་དུད་འགྲོ་དང་། ཙི་ཤིང་ནགས་ཚལ་ཆུའི་ཐོན་ཁུངས་སོགས་མདོར་ན། རང་བྱུང་ཁམས་ཡོངས་རྫོགས་འགྲོ་བ་མེར་དགོས་མཁོ་ཡོད་ལ་ལས་འགན་ཀྱང་ཡོད་པའི་ཀོར་ནང་ཆོས་ཀྱི་གཞུང་ནས་གསུངས་པའི་བསླབ་བྱ་རྣམས་ཕྱོགས་བསྒྲིགས་བྱས་ནས་འགྲེམས་ཕེལ་དྲ་རྒྱ་ཡིན་པ་ཐར་བྱུང་མ་མྱོང་བ་ཞིག་རེད།

ནང་ཆོས་ཀྱི་ནགས་ཚལ་རྟག་པོ་དང་། དགོན་གནས་སུ་གནས་པའི་སྒོམ་ཆེན་སོགས་ལ་གལ་ཆེ་རྩིས་པ་དང་། དེ་བཞིན་རི་དྭགས་དང་ཙི་ཤིང་སོགས་མང་པོ་སྲོག་ཆགས་ཀྱི་རིགས་རྣམས་དཔེ་རྒྱུན་ཇི་འདྲ་ཞིག་ཆོས་རྫས་ཀྱིས་མཆོད་བྱེད་དུ་འཛིན་པ་རྣམས་ལ་རང་བྱུང་ཁམས་སྲུང་སྐྱོབ་བྱེད་རྒྱུའི་བསླབ་བྱའི་ཡིག་ཆ་རྒྱ་ཆེ་འཚོལ་སྒྲུབ་བྱེད་ཐུབ་པ་དེར་ཡ་མཚན་ཀྱིས་དགོས་པའི་རྒྱུ་མཚན་གང་ཡང་མེད་པ་ཞིག་རེད།

རབ་བྱུང་རྣམས་ཤིང་གཅོད་མི་ཆོག་པ་རེད། དེ་ཡང་ཚང་མས་ཤེས་གསལ་ལྟར་ཇོན་ཀྱ་པ་ཞིག་གིས་ཤིང་སྡོང་གི་ཡལ་ག་ཞིག་བཅད་པའི་རྗེས་སུ་ཤིང་དེར་གནས་པའི་ལྷ་དེས་ཁོ་རང་གི་བུའི་ལག་པ་ཡ་གཅིག་བཅད་སོང་ཞེས་བཅོམ་ལྡན་འདས་ལ་དེ་ཞུས་པའི་ལོ་རྒྱུས་ཡོད་པ་རེད།

ཡང་ལོ་རྒྱུས་ཀྱི་བསླབ་བྱ་གཞན་ཞིག་ལ་ཐར་འགྲུལ་པ་འགའ་ཞིག་བྱང་ཆུབ་ཇོན་ཤིང་དེས་སྐྱོགས་པོ་ཐར་འགྲུལ་པ་རྣམས་ལ་ཉི་མ་ཚ་བའི་སྐབས་གྲིབ་གསིལ་སྤྲད་པའི་ཕན་འབྲས་དེར་སྐྱོགས་པོ་དེར་གནོད་པ་བྱས་པའི་བྱ་སྤྱོད་ངན་པ་དེར་ཀུན་འཛུགས་བྱས་ཡོད་པ་རེད།

ཨན་གུ་ཏ་ར་ ནི་ཀཱ་ཡའི་ཕུག་དཔེའི་ནང་། དེ་དང་འདྲ་བའི་ལོ་རྒྱུས་ཤིག་ཡོད་པ་རེད། ཐར་ར་ཛ་ཀོ་རན་ཡ་ཞེས་པ་ཞིག་ལ་བྱང་ཆུབ་ཇོན་ཤིང་ཆེན་པོ་ཞིག་ཡོད་པ་དེའི་མིང་ལ་བརྟན་པོ་ཞེས་ཟེར་ཞིང་། ཤིང་དེའི་ཡལ་ག་རྒྱ་ཆེ་ལ་རིང་ཚད་དཔག་ཚད་བཅུ་གཅིག་ཙམ་ཡོད་པའི་གྲིབ་གསིལ་ཕན་

པ་ཞིག་ཡོད། ཤིང་དེའི་འབྲས་བུ་རྣམས་ལ་སྲུང་བུ་བྱེད་དགོས་པ་མ་ཟད། འབྲས་བུ་ཟས་རྗེས་ཤིང་དེར་གནོད་སྐྱོན་གཏོང་མཁན་ལུ་ཡང་ཡོད་པ་མ་རེད། ཉིན་གཅིག་མི་ཞིག་ཡོང་ནས་ཤིང་དེའི་འབྲས་བུ་རྒྱུག་ཚད་ཟས་རྗེས་ཡལ་ག་གཅིག་ཀྱང་བཅག་ནས་ཕྱིན་པ་རེད། ཤིང་དེར་གནས་པའི་ལྷ་དེའི་བསམ་ཚུལ་ལ། རང་གི་འདོད་པ་འཁེངས་པའི་འབྲས་བུ་ཟས་རྗེས་ཤིང་དེའི་ཡལ་ག་ཡང་བཅག་པ་དེ་འདྲའི་མི་ངན་པ་ལ་ཀ་བསམས་པ་རེད། གལ་སྲིད་ཤིང་སྡོང་དེར་འབྲས་བུ་མ་ཀྱིས་པ་ཡིན་ན་བསམས་ཀ་བས་རྗེས་སུ་ཤིང་དེར་འབྲས་བུ་ཅི་བ་ནས་ཀྱིས་མེད་པ་རེད།

དེ་འདྲ་བའི་ནང་ཆོས་ཀྱི་བསླབ་བྱའི་ཐོག་ནས་ཀྱ་པ་དང་། ཀྱི་པོ་རྣམས་ལ་རྩི་ཤིང་གི་རིགས་དེ་དག་མི་ཙམ་མ་ཡིན་པར་ནགས་གསེབ་ཏུ་གནས་པའི་རི་དྭགས་སོགས་ལའང་ཟས་དང་། བསིལ་གྲིབ་དང་སྲུང་སྐྱབ་སོགས་ཀྱི་ཕན་ཐོགས་ཡོད་པར་བརྟེན་དེ་ཚོར་གནོད་འཚེ་བྱེད་རྒྱུ་མེད་པའི་ལམ་སྟོན་བྱེད་ཀྱི་ཡོད་པ་རེད།

ནགས་ཚལ་ལ་ཅིས་མཐོང་ས་དུས་པར་ནགས་ཚལ་རྒྱ་ཆེན་པོ་རྩ་མེད་བཟོས་པའི་རྐྱེན་གྱི་དེང་སང་ས་རུལ་རྒྱབ་པ་དང་ཆུ་རག་མེད་པའི་རྐྱེན་གྱི་མཐའ་ས་ས་ཞིང་ལ་གནོད་འབྲས་ས་ཞིན་པ་དང་། སྤྲུག་ཆགས་དང་རྩི་ཤིང་རིགས་རྣམས་ཀྱང་གནས་ཡུལ་མེད་པའི་རྐྱེན་གྱི་རྩ་ཟད་དུ་འགྲོ་གི་ཡོད་པ་རེད།

ལོ་ ༡༥༠༠ ཛན་མི་དང་། རང་བྱུང་ཁམས་དབར་མཉམ་གནས་ཀྱི་སྐྱི་ཚོགས་ཞིག་ནང་ནང་པ་སྒྲུབ་པའི་ཆོས་དེ་རྩ་བ་ཚུགས་པ་ཞིག་ཡིན་ནའང་། འཛམ་གླིང་འདིའི་རང་བྱུང་ཁམས་ཐོག་ལ་སྐྱོན་ངན་པ་བྱུས་ན་དེའི་འབྲས་བུ་ཇི་འདྲ་ཡོང་མིན་དུས་སྐབས་དེ་ནས་གསལ་པོ་ཤེས་ཀྱི་ཡོད་པ་རེད། དཔེར་ན་བྲམ་ཟེའི་ལོ་རྒྱུས་ཞིག་ནང་། བྲམ་ཟེ་རིས་སྟོན་པ་བཅོམ་ལྡན་འདས་ལ་མི་འཕར་ཉིང་དུ་འགྲོ་བའི་རྒྱུ་མཚན་ཇི་ཡིན་བཀའ་དྲིས་ཞུས་སྐབས། སྟོན་པས་གསུངས་གསལ། མི་རྣམས་ཁྲིམས་མེད་འདོད་ཆགས་ཀྱི་མེ་རྩེ་འབར་བ་དང་། མ་རུང་བའི་རི་འདུན་གྱིས་འཁེངས་ཤིང་།། ཆུ་བུ་ཐོག་པར་རྗེས་འདྲངས་ཀྱིས་སྡོངས་སུ་བཅུག་པའི་རྐྱེན་གྱི་གནམ་ནས་ཆར་པ་དུས་ཐོག་མ་བཏང་བ་དང་། ལོ་ཏོག་རྒྱ་ཡང་ཁག་པོ་ཡོད་པ་དང་ལོ་ཏོག་ཞན་ལ། ནད་ཐོགས་པ་སོགས་ ཇི་ཙམ་ལས་ཀྱིས་མི་ཐབ་པར་བརྟེན་མི་གྲངས་ཉུང་དུ་འགྲོ་གི་ཡོད་པ་རེད།

ནང་ཆོས་ཀྱི་གཞུང་ནང་སྡུག་བཅད་བཞའ་གཙོད་རྒྱའི་ཀུན་སློང་འཁྱེར་བ་ཅན་གྱི་མི་དགེ་བའི་ལས་བསགས་ཀྱི་ཡོད་པར་བརྟེན་ནང་ཆོས་ཉམས་ལེན་གཏིང་ཟབ་གནང་མཁན་ཚོས་ཤིང་ཛོག་དང་།

ཚལ། འབྲུ་སོགས་ལ་འཚོ་བའི་ཡ་བྱད་འོངས་སུ་བྱུང་ནས་ལུད་རྫོགས་ཉམས་ལེན་གནང་གི་ཡོད་པ་རེད། དེ་རྒྱ་བུའི་འབྲས་བུས་ཛོན་ཤིང་དང་། འབྲུ་སོགས་ལ་གནོད་འཚེ་བྱེད་རྒྱུ་མེད་པ་ཞིག་རེད།

ནང་ཆོས་ཀྱི་གཞུང་ནས་འཛིག་རྟེན་འདིའི་སྟེང་འགྲོ་བ་མིའི་རིགས་ནི་དམིགས་བསལ་གྱི་གལ་གནད་ཡིན་པ་ཞིག་ཅིས་ཀྱི་ཡོད་པ་རེད། དེ་ནི་འགྲོ་བ་མིར་རྣམ་དཔྱོད་ཀྱི་ཐོག་ནས་ཐག་གཅོད་བྱེད་རྒྱུ་ཡོད་པ་དེ་ཡིན།

འཛམ་གླིང་གི་ས་ཕྱོགས་འགར་གང་ཟག་འགའ་ཞིག་ཚལ་རིགས་རྐྱང་པའི་ཟས་ཀྱིས་ལུས་རྩོལ་བས་ཉམས་པས་རྐྱེན་གྱི་སེམས་ཀྱི་ནུས་པ་དང་ཡར་རྒྱས་འགྲོ་རྒྱུར་གནོད་ཀྱི་ཡོད་པ་རེད། དེ་འདྲར་བརྟེན་ནང་ཆོས་ཀྱི་ཐོག་ནས་ཟས་ཟ་ཆོག་མི་ཆོག་གེར་སོགས་བཅའ་ཁྲིམས་བྱས་ཤིང་། གསལ་བ་ཡོད་པ་དེ་དག་ཞིབ་འཇུག་གི་ཚན་ནས་བརྟག་ཞིབ་བྱེད་བཞིན་རེད། དེབ་འདི་འདྲ་བའི་ངོ་སྤྲོད་རྩོམ་བསྒྲིགས་ཁག་གི་ནང་དོན་སྙིང་པོ་ནི། འགྲོ་བ་མིའི་བྱ་སྤྱོད་མཐའ་དག་རང་བྱུང་འཁོར་ཡུག་ལ་བསྲུང་བཅོ་དགོས་པ་ལས་རང་འདོད་ཀྱིས་རྩ་མེད་བཟོ་མི་རུང་བའི་བསླབ་བྱ་བསྟན་གྱི་ཡོད་པ་རེད།

ནང་ཆོས་ཐོག་ནས་སྲོག་ཆགས་ཚང་མ་ཉིན་གཅིག་ཐར་པའི་ལམ་དུ་འགྲོ་རྒྱུའི་གོ་སྐབས་ཡོད་པ་ཞིག་ལ་ངོས་འཛིན་བྱེད་ཀྱི་ཡོད་པ་རེད། འགྲོ་བ་མི་རྣམས་མཐོ་རིས་ཀྱི་གྲུབ་སུ་ཡོད་ནའང་རང་བྱུང་ཁམས་དང་། སྲོག་ཆགས་སོགས་ལ་དབང་བསྒྱུར་བྱས་པར་འགྲོ་བ་མིའི་རིགས་རྣམས་ཉིན་ཁའི་ནང་སྐྱོང་བའི་བྱ་སྤྱོད་ཞིག་ཡིན་པར་ངོས་འཛིན་བྱེད་ཀྱི་ཡོད་པ་རེད། ནང་ཆོས་ཐོག་ནས་རང་བྱུང་ཁམས་ལ་ཚ་ཕྱོགས་ཕོད་པའི་ཉམས་ཞིབ་པ་ཀུ་ཤ་བས་ཀ་ཚ་དགེ་ལེགས་གཡུ་ཐོག་ནས་ཐེག་པ་ཆེན་པོའི་གཞུང་ནས་སེམས་ཅན་ཐམས་ཅད་ལ་བྱམས་སྙིང་རྗེ་དགོས་པའི་སྐོར་སྤྱག་ཟུར་བཀོད་ཞུས་པ་གཤམ་གསལ།

སྟོན་པའི་ཆོས་དེ་རྩ་བ་སྙིང་རྗེ་ཡིན། དེ་ལ་སྐྱབས་བཅོལ་གང་ཟག་སུ་ཞིག་གིས།
སེམས་ཅན་གཞན་ལ་སྙིང་རྗེའི་བསླབ་སྡོམ་གྱིས། གནོད་པ་འཚེའི་ལས་ཀྱི་བྱ་བ་བྱེད་མི་རུང་།

དེ་བཞིན་སེམས་ཅན་གཞན་ལ་གནོད་འཚེ་བྱེད་རྒྱུ་སྤངས་དགོས་པའི་སྐོར་རྗེ་ཙོང་ཁ་པ་ཆེན་པོས།

སེམས་ཅན་ལ་གནོད་འཚེ་བྱ་རྒྱུའི་བསམ་སྦྱོར་གཉིས་ཀའི་ཐོག་ནས་སྤངས་དགོས་པ་ཞིག་ཡིན། དེ་ཡང་མི་དང་དུད་འགྲོ་སོགས་བརྡུང་བ་དང་། ཐག་པས་བཙམས་པ་དང་། བཙོན་དུ་བཙུག་པ། རྣ་ཁུག་ཏུ་ཤོག་གསང་བཏོན་པ། སེམས་ཅན་དེའི་ལུས་སྟོབས་ཀྱིས་ནུས་ཤུགས་ལས་ལྷག་པའི་ཁལ་ཆེན་པོ་བཀུར་བའི་སྤྱོད་པ་ལ་སོགས་བྱེད་མི་རུང་ཞེས་གསུངས།

དེ་བཞིན་རྫོགས་ཆེན་དཔལ་སྤྲུལ་འཇིགས་མེད་དབང་པོའི་ཀུན་བཟང་བླ་མའི་ཞལ་ལུང་ནང་། ཆོས་ལ་སྐྱབས་བཅོལ་བའི་རྗེས་སུ་སེམས་ཅན་གཞན་ལ་གནོད་འཚེ་སྤོང་དགོས་པ་ཡིན། དེ་ཡང་གནོད་འཚེའི་ལས་ཀ་ནི་རང་གི་མི་ལམ་དུ་འཁོར་མི་རུང་བར་བརྟེན། ལས་དེ་རིགས་སྤོང་ཐབས་སུ་འབད་བརྩོན་བྱེད་དགོས་ཞེས་གསུངས་ཡོད། སེམས་ཅན་གཞན་ལ་གནོད་འཚེ་སྤོངས་རྒྱུ་དེ་ནི་ནང་པའི་སྐྱེས་བུ་དམ་པ་རྣམས་ཀྱིས་བྱམས་པ་དང་། སྙིང་རྗེ། གཞན་ཕན་སོགས་ཀྱི་སྤྱོད་སོགས་ལ་བརྟེན་པའི་ཐོག་མ་དེ་ཡིན། སྟོན་པ་བཅོམ་ལྡན་འདས་ཀྱིས་བྱམས་བརྩེ་དེ་གལ་ཆེ་ཡིན་པའི་སྐོར་གསུངས་ཡོད།

འཛམ་གླིང་བྱེ་བ་མང་པོའི་རྒྱུ་ནོར་ཕུན་སུམ་ཚོགས་ལ་རྒྱུ་ཆེ་བའི་མཆོད་པ་དུས་རྟག་ཏུ་དཀོན་མཆོག་གསུམ་ལ་ཕུལ་བ་དེ་སྐད་ཅིག་ཙམ་གྱི་བྱམས་སྙིང་རྗེ་བྱས། དེའི་ཕན་ཡོན་དང་འགྲན་མི་ཐུབ། ཡང་ནང་པའི་ཆོས་ཀྱི་གཙོ་བོ་སྙིང་རྗེ་ཡིན་པ་དཔེ་མཚོན་གཞན་ཞིག་ནས་བརྗོད་ན། ཤ་མས་རང་གི་སྡུག་ལ་ཐུག་ཀྱང་། སོ་སོའི་བུ་གུ་སྐྱོང་སྐྱོབ་བྱེད་ཀྱི་ཡོད་པ་བཞིན་ཚང་མས་གཞན་གྱི་སྡུག་ཀྱང་སོ་སོའི་སྡུག་དང་མཚུངས་པའི་བསམ་བློ་གཏོང་དགོས་པ་ཡིན།

ལོ་ཉིས་སྟོང་ལྔ་བརྒྱའི་གོང་ནས་སྟོན་པ་སངས་རྒྱས་བཅོམ་ལྡན་འདས་ཀྱིས་འཛམ་གླིང་འདི་དང་། སྟོང་གསུམ་གྱི་སྟོང་ཆེན་པོའི་ཕྱིའི་འཇིག་རྟེན་གྱི་ཁམས་དང་། ནང་བཅུད་ཀྱི་སེམས་ཅན། བར་སྣང་གི་སྣང་ཁམས་སོགས་འཇིག་རྟེན་བཀོད་པའི་ཆགས་ཚུལ་སོགས་ནང་ཆོས་ཀྱིས་གཞུང་ནས་གསུང་པ་མང་པོ་ཞིག་དེང་སང་གི་ཚན་རིག་པས་བརྟག་དཔྱད་བྱས་ཏེ་ཤེས་ཚོར་བྱུང་ནས། ད་ལས་རྟོགས་བྱེད་ཀྱི་ཡོད་ཀྱང་། ནང་པས་དེ་ཚོར་གལ་ཆེ་མི་འཛིན་པར། དེ་ལས་འཕྲོ་བ་ཤི་རྣམས་གཞན་ཕན་སྙིང་རྗེ་ཆེན་པོའི་བསླབ་བསྡོམས་སྲུང་རྒྱུ་དེ་གལ་གནད་ཆེ་བ་ཅིས་ཀྱི་ཡོད།

དེང་སང་ཆུ་སྒྲིགས་མ་ཆགས་པའི་རྒྱུན་གྱི་མིའི་འཕྲོད་བསྟེན་དང་། སྲོག་ཆགས་མང་པོ་ཞིག་ལ་གནོད་སྐྱོན་ཡོང་གི་ཡོད་པ་དེ་དག་ལོ་བརྒྱ་ཕྲག་སྔོན་ནས་སྟོན་པ་བཅོམ་ལྡན་འདས་ཀྱིས་ཆུ་སྒྲིགས་བཟོ་མི་ཆོག་པའི་འདུལ་བའི་བཅའ་ཁྲིམས་གཏན་འབེབས་གནང་ཡོད་པ་དང་། དེ་བཞིན་ཐ་ན་གསང་སྤྱོད་རྒྱབ་ཧ་ངས་ཡན་ལག་བཅའ་ཁྲིམས་གཏན་འབེབས་གནང་བ་དེ་དག་རང་བྱུང་ཁམས་སྲུང་སྐྱོབ་དགོས་པར་གལ་གནད་ཆེན་པོ་ཅིས་གནང་བ་ཞིག་རེད།

ནང་ཆོས་ནས་རང་བྱུང་ཁམས་དར་ཁྱབ་ཡོང་རྒྱུར་ཤུགས་གནོན་སྟོན་པ་མ་ཟད། ནང་ཆོས་ཀྱིས་རང་བྱུང་ཁམས་ལ་དཔེ་མཚོན་བྱུར་ནས་བསླབ་བྱ་མང་པོ་རྒྱབ་ཀྱི་ཡོད་པ་རེད། དཔེར་ན།

རྙོགས་མའི་རྫིང་བུ་ཞིག་དཀྲུགས་ན་འདམ་ཡོད་པས་གསལ་བར་མི་རུང་བ་བཞིན་སེམས་

ཀྱང་། དེ་བཞིན་སྐོགས་མར་གནས་པ་ཡིན། གལ་ཏེ་གཙང་ཞིང་འཛམ་པའི་རྫོང་བུ་ཞིག་མ་དཀྲུགས་པར་གང་ཟག་གི་ཆུའི་ནང་གི་རྡོ་དང་། ༡། འགྲོན་བུ། དུང་དཀར་སོགས་གསལ་བར་མཐོང་བ་བཞིན་སེམས་ཀྱང་དེ་བཞིན་ཞི་བདེར་གནས།

མེ་ཏོག་པདྨ་དེ་བཞིན་ཉིན་རྫུ་དང་། ནང་པ་གཉིས་ཀྱིས་ཉོན་མོངས་དུས་གསུམ་གྱི་མ་འགོས་པར་ཞེས་བྱ་ཡོན་ཏན་གྱི་དཔེ་མཚོན་དུ་རྩིས་ཏེ་རྩ་ཆེར་འཛིན་གྱི་ཡོད་པ་རེད། དཔེར་ན།

མེ་ཏོག་པདྨ་སྔོན་པོ་དང་། དམར་པོ། དཀར་པོ་སོགས་འགའ་ཤས་འདམ་རྒྱུའི་ནང་ཀྱིས་ཏེ་ཡར་ཐོན་མ་ཐུབ་པར་འདམ་རྒྱུ་དེའི་ནང་བསིམས་ནས་ཐད་ཀྱི་ཡོད་པ་རེད། དེའི་ནང་ནས་མེ་ཏོག་པདྨ་འགའ་ཤས་ཡར་ཐོན་ཏེ་འདམ་མ་གོས་པར་གཙང་ཞིང་དྲི་ཞིམ་དང་ལྡན་པ་ཞིག་ཡོད་པ་རེད།

དེ་བཞིན་བཅོམ་ལྡན་འདས་ཀྱི་གསུང་ཆོས་ནང་། ཀ་ག་དང་གླུ་ཆེན། སེང་གེ་སོགས། དཔེ་མཚོན་དུ་སྦྱར་ནས་བསླབ་བྱ་མང་པོ་གནང་ཡོད་པ་རེད། དཔེར་ན།

ཡིག་ཆ་འགའ་ཤས་ནང་ཁོང་གི་སེང་གེའི་ངར་སྒྲ་ཀ་བུ་སྲོག་ཆགས་འབུ་བསྲིང་ཆུང་དུ་ཙམ་ལའང་གནོད་འཚོ་བྱེད་མི་ཉན་པའི་བསླབ་བྱ་གསུང་གི་ཡོད་པ་རེད།

ཆེས་ཐ་མོ་ནས་སྲོག་ཆགས་ཀྱི་རིགས་འགའ་ཞིག་འཚོ་གནས་ཐུབ་མིན་གྱི་ཉེན་ཁ་ཡོད་པ་དང་། སྲོག་ཆགས་རྣམས་མེད་པར་འགྱུར་ན་འཛམ་གླིང་སྣོད་བཅུད་ཀྱི་ནུས་པ་ཉམས་ཆགས་འགྲོ་གི་རེད། ནང་ཆོས་ཀྱི་དཔེ་ཆའི་ནང་། མི་དང་རི་དྭགས་བར་ཚུན་བརྟེན་འབྱུང་གི་འབྲེལ་བ་ཡོད་པ་རེད། ཅེས་གསལ་ཡོད། དབྱིན་ཡུལ་གྱི་རྒྱལ་ས་ལོན་ཊོན་དུ་ཡོད་དུ་ཡོད་པའི་ པ་ལི་ཡི་གེའི་ཚོགས་པ་ནས་ . ཁུད་ད་ཀ་པ་ཐ་ (Khuddakapatha) ཞེས་པའི་དཔེ་ནས་གཤམ་གྱི་ཚིགས་བཅད་འདི་བཞིན་ཟུར་བཏོན་གནང་ཡོད།

སྐྱེ་ས་ཏ་ག་རྣམས་ནགས་ལུ་ཚུར་སྤྲོག་དང་།
ཁྱེད་ཅག་མེད་ཚེ་ནགས་ཚལ་སྟོང་པར་ཟད།
དེ་རྗེས་ཁྱེད་ཞང་གནས་ཡུལ་སྟོང་འགྱུར་བས།
དེ་ཕྱིར་ནགས་རྣམས་སྐྱབ་ཕྱིར་མཐོ་བསམས་མོང་།

ནང་ཆོས་ནི་དུས་རྟག་ཏུ་འཛམ་བུ་གླིང་འདིའི་རིག་གནས་ཀུན་ནས་ཕྱུག་པོས་ར་ཆེན་པོ་ཞིག་ཏུ་གནས་ཡོད། དཔེར་ན། མེ་ཏོག་པདྨ་དེ་རྩི་ཤིང་ཀུན་ནས་ཁྱུ་མཆོག་ཏུ་འགྱུར་བ་བཞིན་ཡིན།

ནང་པའི་བསྟན་བཅོས་ཚང་མའི་ནང་ཐུབ་པ་བཅོམ་ལྡན་འདས་ནགས་ཚལ་དུ་ཚལ་གྱི་སྤོག་འོག་ཏུ་སྐུ་བལྟམས་པར་བཤད་ཡོད། ལོ་རྒྱུས་ལ་གཞིགས་ན་ཁོང་འཁྲུངས་མ་ཐག་གོམ་བདུན་སྤོས་ནས་མེ་ཏོག་པདྨ་བདུན་འཁྲུངས་པ་རེད། ཡུཛ་ནི་ཡི་ཤིང་གི་གྲིབ་བསིལ་འོག་གཞོན་ནུའི་དུས་ཀྱི་ཉིང་དེས་འཛིན་ལ་ཐོབ་པའི་སྐབས་དེའི་གཡས་གཡོན་དུ་ཤིང་དེ་ ཉིང་ ༨༥༠ ཙམ་ཡོད།

དེ་རྗེས་བྱང་ཆུབ་ལྗོན་ཤིང་གི་ཡལ་འདབ་རྒྱས་པའི་འོག་སྟོན་པ་སངས་རྒྱས་ཀྱི་གོ་འཕངས་བརྙེས་པ་རེད། བྱང་ཆུབ་ཀྱི་ལྗོན་ཤིང་དེ་བཞིན་ནང་པར་རྩ་ཆེན་ཡིན་ཙམ་མ་ཟད། ཕྱི་རོལ་མུ་སྟེགས་པའི་ཆོས་ལུགས་པ་རྣམས་ཀྱིས་ཀྱང་རྩ་ཆེར་རྩིས་པ་རེད།

དཔེ་མཚོན་དེ་དག་ལས་ང་ཚོས་རྩི་ཤིང་འདི་རིགས་ཆོས་ཀྱིས་སྲུང་སྐྱོབ་བྱེད་དགོས་པ་མངོན་ཐུབ་པ་ཡིན། གང་ཡིན་ཟེར་ན། དེ་དག་ནི་སྟོན་པ་སངས་རྒྱས་བཅོམ་ལྡན་འདས་ཀྱི་མཛད་པ་རྣམས་ཐར་མཚོན་ཐུབ་པའི་དཔེ་མཚོན་རྩ་ཆེན་ཤ་སྟག་ཞིག་རེད། དད་ལྡན་རྣམས་དེ་ལ་ཆེད་མངགས་གནོད་འཚེ་བྱ་མི་རིགས་པ་ཡིན།

ཉམས་ཞིབ་བྱེད་མཁན་ཚོར་ཁྱད་ཚོར་པོ་ཞིག་ཤེས་རྟོགས་ཡོང་རྒྱུར་རང་བྱུང་ཁམས་ལ་འགྲེལ་བཤད་རྒྱབ་སྟངས་ཕྱོགས་གཉིས་ནས་བྱེད་ཀྱི་ཡོད། དངོས་མཐོང་གི་འགྲེལ་བརྗོད་གཅིག་དང་ཕྱོགས་རེ་འགའ་བའི་འགྲེལ་བརྗོད་གཅིག་བཅས་ཡོད།

དེ་དག་ང་ཚོས་རྒྱ་གར་བྱང་ཕྱོགས་ཀྱི་རྫོང་ཁག་ཞིག་གི་རང་བྱུང་ཁམས་ཀྱི་འཁོར་ཡུག་གི་གནས་དང་ཡུན་ལས་ལེན་པ་ཡིན་གཤིས། དེ་དག་སྔ་ཕྱིས་ཀྱི་ནུས་པ་ཁྱད་འཕགས་ཅན་གྱི་རྟེན་འབྱུང་ལས་བྱུང་བ་ཞིག་ཀྱང་ཡིན། ཕ་མོའི་ནང་པ་རྣམས་རང་བྱུང་རིག་པར་དགའ་མོས་ཡོད་ཚ་ཞིག་ནི་ངེས་པར་ཡིན།

དེ་ཡང་སྔོན་པས་མདོ་ལུ་ཏ་ནི་པ་ཏ་ལས་རྩི་ཤིང་དེ་དག་གི་བརྒྱུད་ལ་རིགས་མི་འདྲ་བ་རྣམ་པ་ཇི་ཙམ་འདུས་ཡོད་པ་སོགས་དངོས་སུ་མངོན་ནུས་པ་རྣམས་བདག་ཅག་གིས་རྟོགས་པར་བྱ་དགོས།

དེ་བཞིན་འབུ་དང་། སྦུག་པའི་འབུ། ཕྲུག་མ་སོགས་ཀྱང་རིགས་མི་འདྲ་བ་ཇི་ཙམ་ལས་བརྡུས་ཡོད་པ་རྣམས་ཀྱང་ཤེས་དགོས་པ་ཡིན།

ཡུལ་ལྗོངས་ཀྱི་མཐའ་འཁོར་ལ་རྒྱན་ཤིང་ར་ཚོགས་དང་མེ་ཏོག་སོགས་མཛེས་ཤིང་བརྗིད་ཆ་ར་སུ་གནས་པའི་དབུས་ པའི་ཁྲུ་ཚོགས་ཀྱི་མཐར་ལ་རབ་བྱུང་དང་། གོམ་ཆེན་གནས་ཡོད།

ཡུལ་ལྗོངས་ཀྱི་བརྗོད་པའི་བཤད་པར། འབྲས་བུ་འཐག་པའི་ས་གཞི་ལས་རྩི་ཤིང་རྣམས་ལ་མེ་ཏོག་བཀྲ་བ་མིན་ཞིང་ཞེས་དང་། གླང་པོ་དང་། བ་གླང་། ཤ་བ། གཡག སེང་གེ་དང་། སེ་རུ། དེ་རྗེས་སྟག གཟིག་ནག་པོ། དོམ་ལ་སོགས་རི་དྭགས་འདྲ་མིན་མང་པོ་ཡོད།

འཛམ་གླིང་ནང་མིའི་གྲངས་འབོར་ཆེས་འཕར་དང་། དེ་དག་གིས་མི་ཤེས་པའི་ཚོང་སེམས་དང་། འདོད་ཛམ། འཛམ་གླིང་གི་ས་གཞིར་གུས་བཀུར་ཆུང་བ་སོགས་ཀྱིས་རྐྱེན་པས་ཡིད་དགའ་བའི་ཟུམ་ར་དེ་དག་དུག་གི་ངོ་བོར་འགྱུར་ཏེ། རང་བྱུང་རིག་པ་ལ་ཡར་རྒྱས་བྱུང་མེད། དེ་ཕ་བུའི་རང་བྱུང་གི་ཡོན་ཏན་ལ་བརྟོར་བཤིག་གཏོང་མཁན་རྣམས་ལ་ནང་པ་སངས་རྒྱས་པ་རྣམས་ཀྱིས་རྒྱབ་གཉེར་ནས་ཡང་བུ་ཐབས་མེད་གཤིས། ལེགས་བཤད་ཀྱི་ལྟ་གྲུབ་རྒྱས་པར་བྱེད་ཕྱིར་སློབ་གཉེར་བྱེད་མཁན་དང་། མ་འོངས་པའི་མི་རབས་རྣམས་ཀྱི་ཆེད། དེ་དག་གལ་ཆེར་བརྩིས་མཐོང་བྱེད་མཁན་ཚོས་དེ་ལ་ངོ་བསྒོལ་བྱེད་ཀྱི་རེད།

ནང་ཚོས་ཀྱིས་རང་བྱུང་གི་ཁ་བ་ལ་རྟོགས་ཞིབ་ཏུ། ང་ཚོས་ཐབས་ཇུ་ཚོགས་ཀྱིས་གསར་གྲུབ་བྱུས་པ་དང་། བསླབ་བྱ་ཐུགས་བསྒྲིགས་བྱུས་ཡོད་པ་མ་ཟད། དུས་ཡུན་ཐུང་ངུའི་ནང་རང་བྱུང་ཁམས་ལ་གནོད་པ་ཇི་ཙམ་བསྐྱལ་ཡོད་པ་ཡང་ཤེས་ཐུབ། དེ་ནི་གནས་ཀུལ་མང་པོ་ཤེས་རྟོགས་བྱུང་བ་ཞིག་དང་དེའི་ཐོག་ཉམས་ཞིབ་བྱ་རྒྱ་དེ་རྗེ་དྲག་པོ་ཞིག་ཡིན་པ་དང་། དེ་ཙ་ཁ་ལམ་སྔོང་ཡོང་བར་དེའི་ཆེར་སློབ་སྟོན་བྱེད་མཁན་རྣམས་ལ་ཤེས་ཡོན་གྱི་མཐུན་རྐྱེན་འཛོམས་པོ་སྤྲོད་དགོས་པ་ཡིན།

ང་ཚོའི་ངོས་ནས་ཆེས་ཛ་ཚིའི་དུས་ནས་དར་ཁྱབ་བྱུང་བའི་ནང་ཚོས་ཀྱི་གླེགས་བམ་ནང་གསུངས་པ་རྣམས་རང་བྱུང་ཁམས་ཀྱི་སྲུང་སྐྱོབ་ལ་ཕན་ནུས་ཅན་ཞིག་དང་། ཡང་དག་པ་ཞིག་ཡིན་པའི་གོ་ནས། དེའི་གནད་དོན་རྣམས་འཕོངས་སུ་སྤྱོད་ཐབས་བྱེད་དགོས།

ང་ཚོས་ལས་དོན་འདི་དག་གི་འབྲས་བུ་རྣམས་གཞན་གྱི་སྙན་དུ་བཞུགས་ནས་འཁོར་ཡུག་ཀུན་སྤྱོད་རིག་པར་བརྟེན་ནས་མ་ཤེས་པ་རྣམས་ཤེས་པར་བྱ་རྒྱུ་དང་། འདོད་ཛམ་གྱི་ལྟ་ཕན་སེམས་ཀྱིས་མེད་པར་བཟོས། སེམས་ཅན་ཐམས་ཅད་ལ་བྱམས་པ་དང་སྙིང་རྗེའི་ལམ་ནས་འཛིག་བརྟེན་རྫོང་ཀྱི་ཁམས་ལ་རྩིས་མཐོང་ཡོང་ཐབས་བྱ་དགོས་པ་ཡིན་ནོ།།

༄༅། ད་ལྟའི་འཁོར་ཡུག་གི་གནས་སྟངས་དང་མཐོང་བའི་དགོས་མཁོ།

ཉེ་ཏུན།

ང་ སྒྲ ད །

༄༅། འདས་པའི་ལོ་ངོ་བཅུ་ཕྲག་གསུམ་རིང་འཛམ་གླིང་འདིར་ཟར་མ་བྱུང་བའི་གང་ཅིའི་ཡར་ཐོན་བྱུང་ཡོད་རེད། ཐོན་བསྐྱེད་ཀྱི་དངོས་རྫས་ཁྱབ་འཕར་མིན་རྒྱ་ཆེ་བ་ལོངས་སུ་སྤྱད་དང་སྤྱོད་བཞིན་ཡིན་པ་དང་། རིམ་འགྲོས་འདི་ནི་གལ་འགངས་ཅན་གྱི་ཕྱུག་འཚོའི་ལས་སྤྱོད་ཀྱི་རང་བཞིན་རྣམས་དང་ཕྱི་ཁམས་འཁོར་ཡུག་གི་རང་བཞིན་ལ་ཕན་གནོད་འབྲེལ་བ་ཞིག་རེད། འདི་དག་ལས་འགྱུར་འགྲོས་ཁ་ཤས་ལ་བརྟེན་ནས་སླར་ཡང་བསྐྱར་གསོ་བྱེད་ཐབས་བྲལ་བའི་ཚབས་ཆེའི་མཐའ་འབྲས་མང་པོ་ཞིག་འཛམ་གླིང་འདིར་ཡོང་སྲིད་པའི་ཐད་ལ་སེམས་ངལ་ཅི་ཆེ་ཡོད་བཞིན་རེད།

འགྱུར་འགྲོས་ཀྱི་རིམ་ཚད་དང་ད་བར་འགྱུར་ལྡོག་ཕྱིན་ཟིན་པའི་གནས་ཚུལ་རྣམས་མཚོན་བྱེད་དཔེ་གྲངས་དུ་མ་ལས་ཤེས་ཐུབ།

ལོ་རེ་བཞིན་ཞིང་ས་དང་རྩི་ཁ་ཅན་གྱི་ཐང་ས་རྒྱ་ཁྱོན་ཧེག་ཏར་ས་ཡ་ཉི་ཤུ་ཐམ་པ་བྱེ་ཐང་དུ་འགྱུར་བ་དང་། ས་བཅུད་ཆུ་རླུང་གིས་འཁྱེར་བ་དང་། ཞིང་ས་མ་ཡིན་པའི་ཆེད་དུ་སྤྱོད་རྒྱུར་བྱེད་པ། གཞན་ཡང་རྐྱེན་གཞན་མང་པོ་ལ་བརྟེན་ནས་ས་གཞིའི་ཐོན་བསྐྱེད་ནུས་བཅུད་གཏན་མེད་

དུ་གཏོང་བཞིན་རེད།

ལོ་རེ་བཞིན་དྲོད་སའི་ཤིང་ནགས་རྒྱ་ཁྱོན་ཞེག་ཏར་ས་ཡ་བཅུ་གཉིས་ཙམ་བརླག་ཏུ་འགྲོ་བཞིན་རེད།

ལོ་རེ་བཞིན་ནུས་བཅུད་ཅན་གྱི་ཞིང་སཿ ཧེ་ཚད་ཁྱོན་ཚྭ་ཞེར་འབུམ་ཉི་ཤུ་ཙམ་ཟ་ཚྭ་སྣུང་གིས་འཕྲོར་འདེད་བྱེད་བཞིན་རེད།

ལོ་རེ་བཞིན་རང་བྱུང་གཏེར་ཁ་འདོན་སློག་ཆེད་ལ་རྡོ་ ཧེ་ཚད་ཁྱོན་ཏོན་ཞེར་འབུམ་སུམ་སྟོང་ཐམ་པ་ཕྱིར་འདོན་བྱེད་བཞིན་རེད།

ཕྱི་ལོ་ ༡༩༨༠ ནས་ ༡༩༨༥ བར་ཆུའི་བེད་སྤྱོད་འཕར་ཆ་སོང་བ་ཀི་ལོ་མི་ཏར་ཚད་གསུམ་གྱི་བཞི་མ་ ༣༠༠༠ ནས་ ༣༧༥༠ བར་ཕྱིན་ཡོད།

ཚོང་སྒྱུར་བྱེད་པའི་འཕྲུལ་འཁོར་ཞི་རྫས་ཀྱི་མཁོ་སྤྱོད་དེང་སང་ལོ་རེ་བཞིན་མེ་ཊེ་རིག་ཏོན་ས་ཡ་ ༧༥༠༠ སྐོར་བྱེད་ཀྱི་ཡོད་པ་དང་། འདི་ནི་ལོ་ཉི་ཤུའི་གོང་ལས་ཉིས་ལྡབ་ཕལ་ཆེར་རེད།

ལོ་རེ་བཞིན་གཙོ་བོ་ཡར་རྒྱས་འགྲོ་བཞིན་པའི་རྒྱལ་ཁབ་རྣམས་དང་། ཕྱུག་པར་གྲོང་གསེབ་ས་ཁུལ་ཁག་ཏུ་ཁྱིམ་ཚང་གི་མཁོ་སྤྱོད་ཆེད་མེ་ཤིང་ཁྱོན་ཚད་གསུམ་གྱི་བཞི་མ་མི་ཏར་ཞེར་འབུམ་གཉིས་སྐོར་སྤྱད་ཟད་འགྲོ་བཞིན་རེད།

རྣམ་འཁོར་མོ་ཏར་རིགས་ ༡༩༥༠ ལོར་གྲངས་ཁྲིན་ས་ཡ་ལྔ་བཅུ་སྐོར་ཡོད་པ་ལས་ ༡༩༨༧ ལོར་ས་ཡ་ ༩༡༠ ཐུག་ཏུ་འཕར་ཆ་ཕྱིན་ཡོད་རེད།

གྲངས་འཕར་ཤུགས་ཆེ་ཤོས་དེ་ནི་མི་འབོར་རེད། འཛམ་གླིང་གི་མི་འབོར་ཐེར་འབུམ་དང་པོ་དེ་ཕྱི་ལོ་ ༡༨༠༠ ལོ་སྟོད་ལ་ཡིན་ཅིང་། དེ་ནས་ལོ་བརྒྱ་ཐམ་པའི་རྗེས་ལ་ཐེར་འབུམ་གཉིས་པ་ཡིན། དེ་རྗེས་ལོ་ ༣༠ མཇུག་ཏུ་ཐེར་འབུམ་གསུམ་པ་དང་། དེ་ནས་ ༡༩༦༠ ནས་ ༡༩༧༥ བར་ལོ་བཅོ་ལྔའི་ནང་ལ་ཐེར་འབུམ་བཞི་པ་དེ་ཡིན་པ་རེད། དུས་རབས་འདིའི་མཇུག་མཚམས་ལ་མི་གྲངས་ཐེར་འབུམ་དྲུག་སྐོར་ཡོང་གི་རེད།

གང་ཅིའི་འཕར་ཆ་དང་མཁོ་སྤྱོད་ཀྱི་གྲངས་ཅིས་འཇིགས་སུ་རུང་བ་འདི་དག་ལ་བསམས་ཚོ་བསམ་པར་དཀའ་བའི་གནས་སུ་གྱུར་ཡོད། འཛམ་བུའི་ས་གླིང་འདི་ཚོད་ལས་བརྒལ་བའི་བཀོལ་སྤྱོད་ལོག་པ་དུ་མའི་ཉོག་ཏུ་ཚུད་ཡོད་པ་ནི་ཤ་ཅང་གསལ་པོ་རེད། ས་གླིང་བྲེག་གཏུབ་བྱེད་པ། འབུར་འཇོམས་བྱེད་པ། གཞོངས་བསྐང་བྱེད་པ། ནང་བཅུད་བཙིར་དབྱུང་བྱེད་པ། སྐམ་སྲིངས་གཏོང་བ། ཆུ་ལོག་ཀྱིལ་བ། ནགས་ཚལ་གྱི་སྤྲི་བགས་ཁྱོན་ཆེ་བཤུ་བ་བཅས་ལས་ད་ཆ་ས་གཞིའི་རང་བྱུང་བསྐྱར་གསོའི་ནུས་པའང་ཚད་མཐར་གཏུགས་ཟིན་པ་ལྟ་བུར་གྱུར་ཡོད།

རྩོམ་བྲིས་འདིར་ལེ་ཚན་གསུམ་ཡོད། ལེ་ཚན་དང་པོའི་ནང་རླུང་དང་ཆུ་དང་ས་

དང་ཤིང་ནགས་བཅས་ཀྱི་ཐོག་ལ་དཔྱད་པ་མདོར་བསྡུས་ཤིག་བྱས་ཡོད། འདི་དག་ནི་ཕྱིའི་འཁོར་ཡུག་ཉམས་བྱེད་ཀྱི་ཆ་གཙོ་བོ་རྣམས་ཡིན་ཞིང་། སྲོག་ལྡན་རིགས་ཆགས་པ་དང་། ཁྱབ་འཕེལ་ལ་མེད་དུ་མི་རུང་བའི་འཁོར་ཡུག་གི་ཆ་རྣམས་རེད། ཉི་ཚན་གཉིས་པས་རང་བྱུང་འཁོར་ཡུག་ཉམས་བརླག་གི་ལམ་ཕྱོགས་ལས་ཟློག་བྱེད་ཀྱི་དམིགས་བསམ་ཐབས་བྱུས་རིགས་དང་། དཔལ་འབྱོར་དང་ཁྲིམས་འཛུགས་ཀྱི་ལམ་ནས་ཐབས་བྱུས་ཞིབ་ཏུ་མང་པོ་ཡང་ཁོངས་ནས་ཁ་ཤས་ཀྱི་འགྲེལ་བཤད་བྱས་ཡོད།

ཉི་ཚན་གསུམ་པས་སྲོག་ལྡན་འཚོ་བྱེད་ཀྱི་གང་ཅིའི་མཐུད་རྐྱེན་ཡར་རྒྱས་ཆེད་ཐབས་བྱུས་དང་ལས་རགས་གང་དང་གང་ལ་བསམ་གཞིགས་དང་ལག་བསྟར་དགོས་མིན་དང་། འཁོར་ཡུག་ལ་གནོད་སྐྱོན་མི་འགྲོ་བའི་སོ་ནས་རང་བྱུང་ཐོན་རྫས་རྣམས་ལ་ཐབས་མཁས་དང་རྒྱུ་མཚན་ལྡན་པས་ལོངས་སྤྱོད་བྱ་ཚུལ། མདོར་ན་སྲོག་ལྡན་འཚོ་ཐབས་ལ་བསམ་འཆར་འགའ་ཤས་བཅས་བཀོད་ཡོད།

ཡ་རབས་བཟང་སྤྱོད་ཀྱི་སྤྱོད་ཚུལ་སྙིང་རྗེ་དང་བཟོད་པ། སྲོག་ལྡན་ཡོངས་ལ་བརྩེ་སྲུང་བྱེད་པ་སོགས་ལ་ངེས་པར་བདག་སྐྱོང་དང་གཅེས་སྲུས་དགོས་པའི་འབོད་སྐུལ་ཞུགས་ཆེ་དང་། དེ་བཞིན་དུ་དམིགས་བསལ་ཐབས་བྱུས་ཇི་ཡོད་རྣམས་ཀྱི་སྟེང་། ད་ལྟ་དང་མ་འོངས་པའི་མི་རབས་ཡོངས་ཀྱི་ཆེད་ས་གཞིའི་རང་བྱུང་ཐོན་རྫས་རྣམས་ལ་གཅེས་སྲུང་བདག་སྐྱོང་ཆེད་འཛུགས་ཐོག་གི་ཐག་གཅོད་བྱ་ཕྱོགས་བཅས་ཀྱི་ཐད་ལ་འབོད་སྐུལ་དང་བཅས་ཏེ་ཆོས་ཕྱིས་འདི་མཇུག་རྫོགས་བྱས་ཡོད།།

འཁོར་ཡུག་གི་གནས་སྟངས།

༄༅། ཕྱི་ཁམས་འཁོར་ཡུག་གི་གནས་སྟངས་ཇི་འདྲ་ཞིག་ཏུ་གྱུར་ཡོད་མེད་སྐོར་ལ་དེང་སང་གསལ་བསྒྲགས་དང་ཡིག་ཆ་མང་པོ་ཐོབ་ཀྱི་ཡོད། ༡༩༧༢ ལོར་སུ་ཝི་ཌན་གྱི་རྒྱལ་ས་སེ་ཊོག་ཧོམ་ལ་མིའི་ཕྱི་ཁམས་འཁོར་ཡུག་སྐོར་ལ་རྒྱལ་སྤྱིའི་ཚོགས་འདུ་ཚོགས་ཞེས་པ་དེ་ཚོགས་ནས་ལོ་ངོ་བཅུ་སོང་རྗེས་༡༩༨༢ ལོར་རྒྱལ་སྤྱིའི་ཕྱི་ཁམས་འཁོར་ཡུག་ཐོག་མཛད་འཆར་ United Nations Environment Programme, UNEP ཞེས་པ་དེས་འཁོར་ཡུག་གི་གནས་སྟངས་སྐོར་ལ་བསྐྱར་ཞིབ་ཚོག་ཐོ་རྒྱས་ཞིབ་དོན་གསལ་ཅན་ཞིག་ཕྱིལ་ཡོད། མཛད་འཆར་འདིས་ལོ་རེ་བཞིན་འཁོར་ཡུག་གི་གནས་སྐོར་ལ་གལ་ཆེའི་བརྗོད་གཞི་ཆ་ཚོགས་དཔར་བསྐྲུན་བྱེད་ཀྱི་ཡོད་རེད། དེ་བཞིན་དུ་རྒྱལ་ཁབ་སོ་སོ་གཞན་མང་པོ་ནས་ཀྱང་གནས་དོན་འདི་ཐོག་ཉམས་ཞིབ་དང་གསལ་བསྒྲགས་བྱེད་ཀྱི་ཡོད་རེད། དཔྱད་ཞིབ་ཀྱི་ཉི་ཚན་དང་པོ་འདིའི་ནང་ལ་ཙ་བའི་འགྱུར་བ་གང་དང་གང་འགྲོ་བཞིན་ཡོད་པ་གསལ་སྟོན་ཆེད་སྲོག་འཚོའི་ཆ་རྐྱེན་གལ་འགངས་ཅན་ཁག་གི་ལས་ཚུལ་དང་རང་བཞིན་སྐོར་ལ་གོ་བདེའི་ལམ་ནས་འགྲེལ་བཤད་བྱ་རྒྱུ་ཡིན།

བར་སྣང་རླུང་ཁམས་ཀྱི་ཐུས་ཁ།

བར་སྣང་རླུང་ཁམས་ཀྱི་གནས་སྟངས་ཇེ་ཞན་དུ་སོང་བའི་དཀའ་ངལ་མང་པོ་ཞིག་འཕྲད་ཀྱི་ཡོད་རེད། འདི་དག་ནི། དུག་ཚྭའི་བུན་ཆར་ Acid Rain ཞེས་པ་དང་། ཤིང་སྒྲོང་རྫས་རླུང་གི་འདུ་བསགས་ Greenhouse Gases ཞེས་པ་དང་། ཨོ་ཛོན་གྱི་གདན་རིམ་འཕོར་ཟད་ Ozone Layer Depletion ཅེས་པ་སོགས་རེད།

དུག་ཚྭའི་བུན་ཆར་ཞེས་པ་ནི། མུ་ཟི་དང་ན་ཡི་ཏྲོ་ཛན་གཉིས་བར་སྣང་དུ་སྦྱག་འཛིན་རླུང་དང་འདུ་འཕྲོད་བྱས་པ་ལས་གྲུབ་པའི་འདུས་རྫས་ཁྱོན་ཆེ་ཁྱབ་བདལ་དུ་གནས་པ་རྣམས་ཆར་སྤྲིན་གཉིས་དང་འགྲོགས་ཤིང་། དེ་ལ་བརྟེན་ནས་དུག་ཚྭས་བསླད་པའི་གངས་ཆར་ས་ལ་བབས་པ་ལ་ཟེར་བ་རེད། ད་ཆ་རགས་རྩིས་བྱས་ན། མུ་ཟིའི་རྫས་དང་ (Sulphur) ན་ཡི་ཏྲོ་ཛན་ (Nitrogen) གཉིས་ཀྱི་སྦྱག་རླུང་འདུས་རྫས་ (Oxides) ལོ་རེར་ཏོན་ས་ཡ་ ༡༨༠ འཕོ་ཐོན་ཡོང་གི་ཡོད། རྫས་རླུང་འདི་དག་འགྱངས་ཐག་དང་མཐོ་ཚད་ཀྱི་ཀི་ལོ་མི་ཏར་ ༡༠༠༠ རྒྱག་པ་འཕོ་བགྲོད་ཐུབ་ཀྱི་ཡོད་པའང་གསལ་པོར་ཤེས་རྟོགས་ཐུབ་ཡོད། འཕོ་བགྲོད་ཀྱི་རིམ་པའི་སྐབས་མུ་ཟི་སྦྱག་རླུང་ཉིས་འདུས་ (Sulphur dioxide) རྫས་རླུང་ཞེས་པ་དེ་བར་སྣང་ནས་ལམ་ཚུལ་གསུམ་གྱི་སྒོ་ནས་གཙང་ཟད་དུ་འགྲོ་བ་རེད། འོག་གི་ས་གཞིར་ཐིམ་འདུས་ཀྱིས་གཙང་ཟད་དུ་འགྲོ་བ། ཆར་སྤྲིན་གྱི་ཆུ་རྡུལ་ནང་བཞུ་ཐིམ་གྱིས་གཙང་ཟད་དུ་འགྲོ་བ། སྦྱག་འཛིན་རླུང་དང་འདུ་འཕྲོད་ཀྱིས་མུ་ཟིའི་དུག་ཚྭའི་ཆུའི་ (Sulphuric acid) ངོ་བོར་འགྱུར་བས་གཙང་ཟད་དུ་འགྲོ་བ་བཅས་རེད། འདི་དག་རིམ་བཞིན་ཁ་ཆར་དང་འགྲོགས་ཏེ་ས་ལ་བབ་ཀྱི་ཡོད་རེད། ན་ཡི་ཏྲོར་ཛན་དང་སྦྱག་རླུང་འདུས་རྫས་ (Nitrogen oxides) རྣམས་ཀྱང་གོང་བཞིན་འདུས་རྫས་དང་དུག་ཆུའི་ངོ་བོར་སོང་སྟེ་ཁ་ཆར་གྱིས་ས་ལ་འབེབས་ཀྱི་ཡོད་རེད། དེང་སྐབས་ནགས་ཚལ་ཁྱོན་ཆེ་རུ་མེད་དུ་འགྲོ་བཞིན་ཡོད་པའི་རྐྱེན་རྩ་གཙོ་བོ་ཞིག་དུག་ཚྭའི་བུན་ཆར་འདི་རེད་ཅེས་པལ་ཆེར་གྱིས་ངོས་འཛིན་བྱེད་ཀྱི་ཡོད་རེད། དེ་བཞིན་དུ་འདི་ལ་བརྟེན་ནས་རིན་ཐང་བྲལ་བའི་མཁར་རྙིང་དང་སྐུ་བརྙན་རྙིང་རིགས་ཁག་རྙིང་ཟད་དུ་འགྲོ་བའི་མགྱོགས་རྐྱེན་བྱེད་ཀྱི་ཡོད། དེར་བརྟེན་ཙགས་རིགས་རིན་ཆེན་རྡོ་ཚོགས་ལས་གྲུབ་པའི་དངོས་རྙིང་ཁར་དང་མི་འདྲ་བར་བཅའ་དང་གཡའ་ལ་སོགས་པ་ལས་སྲུང་སྐྱོབ་ཆེད་ཚོན་རྩི་ཡང་ཡང་གཏོང་དགོས་སོགས་དཔལ་འབྱོར་གྱི་འགྲོ་གྲོན་ཆེན་མ་མང་པོ་གཏོང་དགོས་འགྱུར་བཞིན་ཡོད་རེད།

ཤིང་སྒྲོང་ཁང་གི་རྫས་རླུང་འདུས་བསགས།

༦༡ སྒྲོང་ཁང་རྫས་རླུང་དེ་ཚོན་ཁོངས་ནས་ཀར་བོན་ཌ་ཡི་ཨོག་ས་ཡིཊ (Carbon dioxide)

དང་། ཀར་བོན་མོ་ནོ་ཨོག་ས་ཡིཊ་ (carbonmonoxide) མི་ཐེན་ (Methane) ན་ཡི་ཊྲོ་ར་ཛན་དང་ཨོག་འཛིན་རླུང་གཉིས་ཀྱི་འདུས་རླུང་ཁག་ (Nitrogen oxides) རྫས་སྦྱོར་ཀྱི་འདུས་བསགས་འཕར་ཆ་ཅི་ཆེར་འགྲོ་བཞིན་ཡོད་པས། འབྱུང་བའི་འགྱུར་འགྲོས་རྫིང་ཁང་འགྱུར་འབྲས་ (Greenhouse Effect) ཞེས་པ་ལ་བརྟེན་ནས་གནམ་གཤིས་ཀྱི་ཚ་དྲོད་རྗེ་མཐོར་འགྲོ་སྲིད། དེ་དག་ལས་ཀྱང་ཀར་བོན་ཌ་ཡི་ཨོག་ས་ཡིཊ་ཐོན་འཕེལ་ཆེ་ཤོས་རེད། ༡༩༥༠ ནས་ ༡༩༨༠ བར་འདིའི་འཕར་ཆ་ལོ་རེ་བཞིན་བརྒྱ་ཆ་བཞིས་ཡར་འཕེལ་དུ་འགྲོ་བཞིན་རེད། བར་སྣང་ལ་ཡོང་གསལ་རྫས་རླུང་ཁག་འཕེལ་བསགས་ལ་བརྟེན་ནས་ཞིང་གསོ་ཁང་གི་འགྱུར་འགྲོས་ལྟར་བར་སྣང་གི་དྲོད་ཚད་འཕེལ་འགྱུར་གཏོང་གི་ཡོད་རེད། ༡༩༨༥ ལོར་ཨ་སེ་ཀྲི་རི་ཡར་རྫིང་ཁང་རྫས་རླུང་དང་གནམ་གཤིས་འགྱུར་འགྲོས་སྐོར་ལ་རྒྱལ་སྤྱིའི་ཚོད་རིག་གི་ལྷན་ཚོགས་ཤིག་གི་སྐབས་སོས་མཐུན་དང་ཤེས་རྟོགས་བྱུང་གསལ། གལ་སྲིད་བར་སྣང་དུ་ཀར་བོན་ཌ་ཡི་ཨོག་ས་ཡིཊ་ཉིས་ལྡབ་ཀྱིས་འཕར་ཆ་བྱུང་ན་ས་སྟེང་གི་ཚ་ཚད་སེན་ཊི་གི་ཊེཊ་ཕྱེད་གཉིས་ནས་ཕྱེད་དང་ལྔའི་བར་འཕར་ཆ་འགྲོ་རྒྱུ་དང་། དེ་ལ་བརྟེན་ནས་རླུང་དང་རྒྱ་མཚོའི་རྦབས་སོགས་ལའང་འགྱུར་བ་འགྲོ་རྒྱུ་དང་། དེ་དག་ལ་བརྟེན་ནས་རྒྱ་མཚོའི་ཁ་ཚད་སེན་ཊི་མི་ཊར་ ༣༠ ནས་ ༡༩༠ བར་མཐོ་རུ་འགྲོ་རྒྱུ་དང་། འདི་དག་དངོས་བྱུང་རྒྱུར་ན་མཚོ་ཁའི་གྲོང་ཁྱེར་མང་པོ་རིམ་བཞིན་མཚོ་འོག་ཏུ་ནུབ་རྒྱུ་སོགས་གནས་ཚུལ་ཚབས་ཆེ་མང་པོ་འབྱུང་སྲིད་པ་རེད།

ཨོ་ཛོན་གྱི་གདན་རིམ་འཐོར་ཟད་ཀྱི་ཉེན་ཁ།

ཨོ་ཛོན་ནི་ (Ozone) རྫས་སྦྱར་འདུ་འཕྲོད་ལ་ཤིན་ཏུ་སྐྱུར་བའི་རྫས་རླུང་ཞིག་རེད། འདི་ནི་བར་སྣང་རླུང་ཁམས་ཀྱི་གདན་རིམ་གཉིས་པ་ཁྱབ་བྱེད་རླུང་ཁམས་ (Stratosphere) ཞེས་པའི་ནང་དུ་གདན་རིམ་སྲབ་མོ་ཞིག་ཏུ་འབྱུང་འཛག་གནས་གསུམ་བྱེད་པ་རེད། ཨོ་ཛོན་གྱི་གདན་རིམ་འདིས་ཉི་ཟེར་གྱི་ཚད་མེད་འོད་ཟེར་ (Ultra Violet) ཞེས་པའི་འོད་ཟེར་དེ་ཐིམ་ལེན་བྱེད་ཀྱི་ཡོད་རེད། འོད་ཟེར་འདི་སྲོག་ཆགས་རིགས་ལ་ཕོག་ན་གནོད་ཚབས་ཆེན་པོ་བྱེད་ཀྱི་ཡོད་བརྟེན་གལ་ཏེ་ཨོ་ཛོན་གྱི་གདན་རིམ་འཐོར་ཟད་དུ་སོར་ན་འོད་ཟེར་འདི་རིགས་ས་སྟེང་དུ་ཐོག་ཕྱིང་གནོད་ཀུན་ཅི་ཆེ་ཡོང་རྒྱུ་རེད། བར་སྣང་གི་ཨོ་ཛོན་གྱི་གདན་རིམ་འཐོར་ཟད་གཏོང་མཁན་གཙོ་བོ་ནི་ན་ཡི་ཊྲོ་ར་ཛན་གྱི་ཨོག་རླུང་འདུས་རྫས་གཉིས་ (NO and NO_2) དང་བར་སྣང་གི་ཆུ་རྡུལ་སོགས་རེད། འོད་ཟེར་འདི་ལ་བརྟེན་ནས་ཀན་སར་པགས་ནད་ (Skin Cancer) རིགས་གཉིས་འབྱུང་སྲིད། མེ་ལ་ནོ་མ་ཞེས་པའི་པགས་ནད་མ་ཡིན་པའི་པགས་ནད་ཀན་སར་ལས་མི་ཀུན་པལ་ཆེར་མི་འབྱུང་ཡང་། མེ་ལ་ནོ་མ་ (Melanoma) པགས་ནད་ཀན་སར་ལས་ནི་ནད་

པ་བརྒྱ་ཆ་ ༣༣ ལ་འཚི་སྐྱོན་གཏོང་བ་རེད།

ཚོད་མེད་འོད་ཟེར་ཞེས་པ་འདི་ས་སྟེང་དུ་ཐོག་འཕོ་ཐང་དུ་སོང་ན། ས་ངོས་ཀྱི་རྩི་ཤིང་ནགས་ཚལ་ལ་འང་གནོད་སྐྱོན་ཆེན་པོ་གཏོང་ནུས། ཨ་རིའི་ལོ་ཉིས་ཉམས་ཞིབ་ཚོགས་པ་ཞིག་གི་ཚོག་ཐོར། བར་སྣང་གི་ཨོ་ཛོན་ཉམས་སྐྱོན་ཕྲན་བུ་ཤོར་བའི་ཡུལ་གྱི་ཟ་དམ་གྱི་ཐོན་ཐག་བརྒྱ་ཆ་ཞེ་བཅུ་ཐམ་པས་ཞན་པ་འདུག་ཅེས་བཀོད་ཡོད་རེད། དེར་བརྟེན་ཅན་ཐོག་ལ་བརྟེན་པའི་དཔལ་འབྱོར་གྱི་གྱོང་གུན་འདི་ཤིན་ཏུ་གལ་འགངས་ཆེན་པོའི་གནས་ཚུལ་ཞིག་རེད། ཁྱབ་ཁྱེད་སྣང་ཁམས་ཀྱི་ཨོ་ཛོན་གདན་རིམ་ལ་ཉམས་འགྱུར་བྱུང་འབྲས་ལས་དྲོད་ཚོད་དང་། སྣང་གི་རྒྱ་བ། ཚ་སྣང་གི་འདུ་གསོག་བཅས་ལ་འང་འགྱུར་བ་ཕྱིན་ཏེ་ས་སྟེང་ཡོངས་ལ་གནམ་གཤིས་ཀྱི་འགྱུར་བ་ཡོང་གི་རེད།

ཆུ་དང་དེའི་བེད་སྤྱོད།

འཛམ་གླིང་ཆུའི་ཁྱབ་ཚད་རགས་རྩིས་ཀི་ལོ་མི་ཊར་ཚད་གསུམ་ཀྱི་བཞི་མ་ས་ཡ་ ༡༩༠༠ ཡོད་ཅིང་འདི་ལ་འགྱུར་བ་ཕལ་ཆེར་མེད། འོན་ཀྱང་ཆུ་ཁྱོན་དེའི་བརྒྱ་ཆ་ ༩༧ རྒྱ་མཚོའི་ཆུ་རེད། བརྒྱ་ཆ་བཅུ་ཟུར་གཅིག་ཙམ་རང་བྱུང་གིས་གཙང་ཆུ་རེད། དེའི་ལྷག་འཕྲོས་རྣམས་འཛམ་གླིང་སྤྲ་བྱུང་གི་མགོ་ཞབས་གཉིས་སུ་འཁྱགས་རོམ་ཐོག་མི་ཊར་ ༧༥༠ མཐུག་ཚད་བར་གནས་པ་དང་། བར་སྣང་གི་ཆུ་རླུང་བཅས་ལ་ཡོད། གཙང་ཆུ་ཁྱོན་ཆུང་འདི་ལས་མེད་པ་དེ་ལ་ཡང་བེད་སྤྱོད་ཐོག་པ་ཡང་ཡང་བཏང་སྟེ་ཆུད་ཟོས་སུ་གཏོང་གི་ཡོད་རེད།

ཆུའི་མཁོ་སྤྱོད།

ཆུའི་མཁོ་སྤྱོད་ཀྱི་རགས་རྩིས་ལྟར་ན། ༡༩༨༥ ལོར་ཆུ་བེད་སྤྱོད་བྱས་པ་ཀི་ལོ་མི་ཊར་ཚད་གསུམ་ཀྱི་བཞི་མ་ ༣༠༠༠ སྐོར་རེད། དེ་ལས་བརྒྱ་ཆ་ ༧༣ ཞིང་ཆུ། བརྒྱ་ཆ་ ༣༡ བཟོ་གྲྭའི་མཁོ་སྤྱོད། བརྒྱ་ཆ་ ༦ ཁྱིམ་ཚང་ནང་གི་མཁོ་སྤྱོད་ལ་ཕྱིན་ཡོད།

༡༩༦༠ ནས་ ༡༩༨༥ བར་ཞིང་ཆུ་འདྲེན་ཡུལ་ས་ཞིང་གི་འཕར་ཆ་ཧེག་ཊར་ས་ཡ་ ༣༨ ནས་ཧེག་ཊར་ས་ཡ་ ༥༠ བར་ཕྱིན་ཡོད། འོན་ཀྱང་ཞིང་ཆུའི་གྲུབ་འབྲས་ནུས་ཤུགས་དམའ་པོ་ལས་ཐོན་ཐུབ་མེད། བརྒྱ་ཆ་ ༣༠ ནས་ ༥༠ བར་མ་གཏོགས་ནུས་ཤུགས་ཐོན་མེད། ཀས་ཤས་ཆེ་སའི་ས་ཁུལ་དུ་ས་འོག་གི་ཆུ་གཏེར་ལ་སྤྱད་ཐལ་ཆེ་བའི་རྐྱེན་གྱིས་ཆུའི་ནུས་བཅུད་རྫོངས་ཟད་དུ་ཕྱིན་པ་དང་། ཆུ་འདྲེན་ལས་ལུགས་མི་འཚམ་པར་སྤྱད་པའི་དབང་གིས་བ་ཚྭ་དང་དུག་ཚྭ་ཅན་དུ་ཤ། །བསྒྱུར་བ་དང་། ཞིང་ས་གཤིན་པོ་རྣམས་ཧ་ཅང་རླན་གཤེར་ཅན་དུ་གྱུར་པ་སོགས་བྱུང་ཡོད་རེད།

བཟོ་གྲྭའི་ནང་དུ་ཆུའི་མཁོ་སྤྱོད་ཕད། ཡར་རྒྱས་ཅན་པའི་རྒྱལ་ཁབ་རྣམས་ནང་བཟོ་གྲྭའི་ནང་ཆུའི་འགྲོ་སྤྱོད་ཆུང་དུ་ཕྱིན་ཡོད། གང་ཡིན་ཞེ་ན། ལས་ལུགས་ཡར་རྒྱས་དང་སྲུང་ཟིན་གྱི་ཆུ་ལ་སྐྱར་ཡང་

སྤྱོད་ཕྱུས་པ་སོགས་ཀྱི་རྒྱུ་མཚན་གྱིས་རེད། འོན་ཀྱང་ཡར་རྒྱས་འགྲོ་བཞིན་པའི་རྒྱལ་ཁབ་ཁག་ནང་བཟོ་ལས་ཡར་རྒྱས་དང་ལྷན་དུ་ཆུའི་མཁོ་སྤྱོད་ཀྱང་ཚ་རུ་འགྲོ་བཞིན་ཡོད་རེད། རྒྱལ་ཁབ་དེ་དག་ནང་ཆུ་ལ་སྤྱོད་མཁས་ཀྱི་ལས་ཚོལ་ཁག་ཡག་ཡོན་བརྩར་དགོས་ཡོད།

མི་མང་གི་འཐུང་ཆུ་དང་། གཙང་སྦྲ། བཀལ་འཕྲུད་བཅས་ལ་ཆུ་འགྲོ་བརྒྱ་ཆ་མི་ཉུང་ཀྱུ་ཆུང་ངུ་ལས་མེད་ཀྱང་། འདི་དག་ནི་འཚོ་བ་མི་རིགས་སྤྱིའི་འཕྲོད་བསྟེན་ལ་ཕན་གནོད་ཆེན་པོ་འབྲེལ་བ་ཞིག་རེད། ཡར་རྒྱས་འགྲོ་བཞིན་པའི་རྒྱལ་ཁབ་ཁག་ནང་མི་གྲངས་ཐེ་ཆ་གསུམ་ལ་འཐུང་ཆུ་གཙང་མ་ཐོབ་དཀའི་དཀའ་ཡོད། མི་འབོར་ཐེར་འབུམ་གཉིས་བཙོག་ཆུ་ཡོངས་སུ་སྤྱད་པ་ལས་བྱུང་བའི་ནད་ཚ་མང་པོའི་ཉེན་ཁའི་འོག་གནས་ཡོད།

ཡར་རྒྱས་འགྲོ་བཞིན་པའི་རྒྱལ་ཁབ་རྣམས་ནང་མི་གྲངས་བཞི་ཆ་གསུམ་ལ་གཞི་རྩའི་གཙང་སྦྲའི་མཐུན་རྐྱེན་རྩ་བ་ནས་མེད།

ཆ་ལ་བཙོག་སྙད་ཀྱི་གནས་ཚུལ།

རྒྱལ་ཁབ་མང་པོའི་ནང་ཁྱིམ་ཁང་གི་བཙོག་ཆུ་དང་། ཞིང་ཆ་ཡས་སྨན་ཡུད་སོགས་ཀྱི་རྐྱེན་གྱིས་ས་སྟེང་ཆུ་གཏེར་རྣམས་ཀྱི་བཙུད་ཤུགས་ལ་འགྱུར་བ་ཆེན་པོ་གཏོང་གི་ཡོད་རེད། ད་བཞིན་དུ་གཙང་ཆུ་རྣམས་དང་ས་འོག་གི་ཆུ་རྣམས་སུ་ན་ཡི་ཏེ་རོ་ཇན་གྱི་འདུས་རྫས་ཕྱིན་ཆེ་འདུས་བསགས་ཡོང་བཞིན་ཡོད་པའང་སེམས་ངལ་འོས་པའི་གནས་ཚུལ་ཞིག་རེད། ཆུ་ལི་ཏར་གཅིག་ནང་དེ་འདྲའི་འདུས་རྫས་མི་ལི་གྲ་རམ་བཅུ་ལྷག་ཡོད་ཚེ་ཕྱུས་པོར་གནོད་ཉེན་ཡོད་རེད།

ཡར་རྒྱས་འགྲོ་བཞིན་པའི་རྒྱལ་ཁབ་ཕལ་ཆེ་བའི་ནང་གྲོང་པའི་བཙོག་ཆུ་རྣམས་གཙང་པོ་དང་རྒྱུགས་ཆུ་རྣམས་སུ་འདྲེས་ཏེ་རང་བྱུང་ཆུ་གཏེར་དེ་དག་འཐུང་ཆུར་མི་རུང་བར་འགྱུར་བཞིན་རེད། བཟོ་གྲྭ་ཡར་རྒྱས་འགྲོ་རིམ་བཞིན་དུ་ཆུར་བཙོག་སྙད་ཀྱང་ཇེ་ཆེར་འགྲོ་བཞིན་རེད། ཕྱིར་བཟོ་གྲྭས་འཐུང་ཆུར་བཙོག་བསྐྱུད་འགོག་ཐབས་གང་ལེགས་མང་པོ་བྱུང་ཡོད་ཀྱང་། ཐབས་ཚུལ་དེ་དག་གིས་འགོག་མི་ཐུབ་པའི་དུག་རྫས་མང་པོ་ཇེ་ཞ། །འཕེལ་དུ་འགྲོ་བཞིན་རེད། དཔེར་ཙམ་བྱས་ན། ཕོ་ལར་རྒྱ་མཚོའི་ནང་རྫས་རིགས་འདྲ་མིན་ཁྲིན་ཐེར་འབུམ་ ༣༥ འཕེན་བཞིན་ཡིན་པ་དང་། དེའི་བརྒྱ་ཆ་ ༡༠ གཙང་ཆུ་བརྒྱུད་ནས་ཡོང་གི་ཡོད།

སའི་གནས་སྟངས།

ད་སྔའི་ཆར་འཛམ་གླིང་ཁྱོན་ལ་ཞིང་ས་རུང་བའི་ས་ཁྱོན་ཧེག་ཊར་ཐེར་འབུམ་ཕྱེད་དང་གཉིས་སོར་ཡོད། རགས་རྩིས་ལྟར་ན། ལོ་རེ་བཞིན་ཞིང་ས་གཤིན་པོ་ཏོན་ཐེར་འབུམ་ ༣༥ རེ་རྩ་བརླག་འགྲོ་བཞིན་རེད། འཛམ་གླིང་ས་ངོས་བརྒྱ་ཆ་ ༩༠ ཕྱེ་ཐང་སྐམ་པོར་འགྱུར་བཞིན་ཡོད། ད་ལ་བརྟེན་ནས་མི་འབོར་ས་ཡ་ ༨༥༠ ལྷག་གི་འཚོ་བའི་གནས་སྟངས་ལ་གནོད་སྐྱོན་ཕྱིན་ཡོད། ལོ་རེ་བཞིན་ཧེག་ཊར་ས་ཡ་ཉི་ཤུ་ནས

བདུན་བར་ཞིངས་ཧུང་བའི་ས་ཁོངས་ནས་བྱེ་ཐང་དུ་འགྱུར་བཞིན་ཡོད།

བྱེ་ཐང་དུ་འགྱུར་གཞིའི་རྐྱེན་རྩ་གཙོ་བོ་ཁག་ནི། རྩྭ་ཁ་ཁག་ལ་སྲུང་སྐྱོང་དགས་པ་དང་། ཞིང་ས་ལ་ནང་གསེས་ཆ་ཕྲན་ཕྲེས་སྐྱགས་པ། ས་འོག་གི་ཆུ་གསེར་རྒྱུན་ཡུད་བྱས་པ། ཞིང་ཆར་པ་ཚྭ་དང་དུག་ཚྭ་རིགས་ཤས་ཆེས་པ། ཤིང་ནགས་དང་རྩྭ་ཤིང་རྣམས་མི་ཤིང་སོགས་ཀྱི་ཚད་བཅད་བཏུབ་མངས་པའི་རྐྱེན་བཅས་རེད།

སའི་སྟུས་ཁ་ཇེ་ཞན་དུ་འགྲོ་བའི་རྒྱུ་རྐྱེན་གཙོ་བོ་ལ། སའི་ནུས་བཅུད་ཡུ་ལྡང་གིས་འཕྱུར་འདོད་བྱེད་པ་དེ་རེད། རྟོན་ཐོག་ཐོན་བསྐྱེད་ལ་ཉམས་རྒུད་འགྲོ་བའི་རྐྱེན་རྩ་གཙོ་བོ་ནི། མི་འབོར་གྲངས་འཕེལ་ཚལ་ཚར་འགྲོ་བའི་དབང་གིས་ཡོད། མི་འབོར་གྲངས་འཕེལ་དང་སྟན་དུ་ས་ཕྱོན་ཆུ་བསྐྱེད་འགྲོ་རྒྱུ་མེད་ཐོག ཐོན་བསྐྱེད་ཀྱི་ཚད་གཞི་དང་སྟུས་ཁ་སོགས་ལ་ཟར་ལས་ཀྱང་ཇེ་ཞན་དུ་འགྲོ་བཞིན་རེད།

རྒྱ་ནག་གི་ཡང་ཅེ་གཙང་པོ་དང་རྒྱ་གར་གྱི་ཆུ་མོ་གང་ག་གཉིས་ཀྱིས་གོ་རིམ་བཞིན་ལོ་རར་བྱེ་མ་ཡོན་ས་ཡ་ ༡༦༠༠ དང་ ༡༩༥༠ འཕྱུར་འདོད་བྱེད་ཀྱི་ཡོད་པ་ཡ་དཔགས་ཏ་ཞིང་ས་རྒྱ་ལྡང་གིས་འཕྱུར་འདོད་ཇེ་ཚམ་འགྲོ་བཞིན་ཡོད་པ་མཚོན་ཐུབ་པ་ཞིག་རེད།

ཤིང་ནགས་འཇོམས་འཇིག་དང་། སྲོག་ཆགས་རིགས་ཆད་སྐོར།

ཚ་དྲོད་ཚ་ལར་ཁྱུ་བའི་ཤིང་ནགས་རིགས་ (Tropical Forests)ནི། འགྲོ་བ་མིར་གང་ཅིའི་ཐད་ནས་༧། །ཤིན་ཏུ་མཁོ་ཕན་ཆེན་པོ་རེད། སྨན་རིགས་བཟོ་གྲྭའི་བརྒྱ་ཆ་ ༥༠ ལྷག་ཤིང་ནགས་འདི་ལས་ཐོན་པ་དང་། གཞན་ཡང་ཀལ་ཆེའི་སྣུམ་རིགས། འཁྱིགས་རིགས། རས་སྦུན། ཚོན་རྩི་དང་སྦྲར་རྩི། ཤིང་རྩི་བཅས་ཀྱང་འདི་ལས་འབྱུང་། གཞན་ཡང་ཤིང་ནགས་འདི་ནི་མི་འབོར་ས་ཡ་ ༣༠༠ སྐོར་གྱི་གནས་ཁང་ལྟ་བུ་དང་། ཁོང་ཚོའི་ལྟོ་ཆས། ཤ་ཤིང་། རྫོད་གནས། སྒོ་ཕྱུགས་ཀྱི་ལྟོ་ཆག་བཅས་ཡོངས་རྫོགས་འདི་ལ་བརྟེན་ཡོད། ད་བར་སྲོག་ཆགས་འདྲ་མིན་རིགས་ས་ཡ་གཅིག་དང་བདུན་འབུམ་སྐོར་ངོས་འཛིན་ཐུབ་ཡོད་ཅིང་། ཡོངས་གྲགས་ལྟར་ན་སྲོག་ཆགས་རིགས་ས་ཡ་ཐེ་ཉུང་མཐར་ཡོད་པར་འདོད་ཀྱི་ཡོད་པ་དང་། ཚན་རིག་མཁས་པ་མང་པོས་སྲོག་ཆགས་རིགས་ས་ཡ་བཅུ་ལྷག་ཡོད་པར་འདོད་ཀྱི་ཡོད་རེད། སྲོག་ཆགས་རིགས་ཕྱེད་ཆེ་དེ་དག་ལས་བརྒྱ་ཆ་ ༧༥ ལས་མི་ཉུང་བ་ཤིང་ནགས་ཀྱི་རིགས་འདིའི་ནང་གནས་ཡོད་རེད།

སྲོག་ཆགས་རིགས་ཆད་ཀྱི་གནས་ཚུལ་ནི། སྔར་དུས་ཀྱི་ཐོག་མ་ནས་བྱུང་ཡོད་ཀྱང་། དེང་སང་སྲོག་ཆགས་རིགས་ཆད་ཀྱི་འཕར་ཚའི་མགྱོགས་ཚད་ལ་བསམ་ན་འཇིགས་སྣང་ཀྱི་འོས་པར་གྱུར་ཡོད། མཁས་པ་ཁ་ཤས་ནས་དུས་རབས་འདིའི་མཇུག་མཚམས་ལ་སྲོག་ཆགས་རིགས་ས་ཡ་གཅིག་ལྷག་སྐོར་གཏན་ནས་རིགས་ཆད་དུ་འགྲོ་རྒྱུའི་མ་འོངས་སྔོན་བརྗོད་བྱས་ཡོད་རེད། སྲོག་ཆགས་ཕྱེད་ཆེ་རིགས་ཆད་དགོས་པའི་རྒྱུ་རྐྱེན་གཙོ་བོ་ཞིག་ནི། སྲོག་ཆགས་དེ་དག་གི་གནས་ཤིང་ནགས་ལྟ་བུ་རྣམས་བསམ་མེད་ཀྱིས་སྟོར་བཅོམ་བྱེད་པ་

དེ་རེད། ཤིང་ནགས་སྐྱོར་བཙོམ་ནི། ཞིང་སའི་ཆེད་ཤིང་ནགས་བྲེག་གཅོད་དང་སྲེག་ཟར་བྱེད་པ། འཐོར་ལམ་བཟོ་བ། གཞིས་ཆགས་འཛུགས་བསྐྲུན་བྱེད་པ། རྒྱ་རགས་བཟོ་བ་སོགས་ལ་བརྟེན་ནས་བྱུང་བའི་གནས་ཚུལ་ཞིག་རེད། དེང་སྐབས་ཤིང་ནགས་བསྐྱར་འདེབས་ཀྱི་ལས་འགུལ་ཅི་ཆེ་བྱེད་བཞིན་ཡང་། ཤིང་ནགས་སྐྱོར་བཙོམ་ཀྱི་ལས་ཤུགས་དེ་ཤིང་ནགས་བསྐྱར་འདེབས་ལས་འགུལ་ལས་ཟློས་བཅུ་སྐོར་གྱིས་ལྷག་པ་ཡོད་རེད། བསྐྱར་འདེབས་བྱེད་པའི་ཤིང་རིགས་ཀྱང་ཕལ་ཆེ་བ་ཁེ་ཚོང་སོགས་ལ་དམིགས་པ་མ་གཏོགས་སྲོག་ཆགས་ཀྱི་བརྟེན་གནས་སུ་རུང་བའི་ཤིང་ནགས་བསྐྱར་གསོ་བྱུང་བ་ཉེས་ཉུང་ངུ་རེད། རགས་རྩིས་བྱས་ན། ལོ་རེ་བཞིན་ཚ་ལྡོང་ཆེ་སར་གྱི་བའི་ཤིང་རིགས་རྒྱ་ཁྱོན་ནེག་ཏར་ས་ཡ་ ༡༢ སྐོར་རྩ་བརླག་ཏུ་འགྲོ་བཞིན་རེད། །

༢་ འཁོར་ཡུག་གི་གནས་སྟངས་ལེགས་བཅོས་ཆེད་ཡར་རྒྱས་ཀྱི་ལས་ཐབས།

ཡར་རྒྱས་ལས་ཐབས་རྒྱ་ཆེ་ཁག་མང་ལག་བསྟར་བྱས་ཡོད་ཅིང་། དེ་དག་བསྡུས་ན། གློག་འཛུགས་དང་། དམིགས་བསལ་ཐབས་བྱུས། དཔལ་འབྱོར་གྱི་ལས་ཐབས་བཅས་རེད།

གློག་འཛུགས་ཀྱི་ཡར་རྒྱས་ལས་ཐབས།

༡༩༧༢ ལོར་གཞུང་གི་གློག་འཛུགས་ཁོངས་འཁོར་ཡུག་སྲུང་སྐྱོབ་ཆེད་བློན་ཆེན་ལྷན་ཁང་དམ་ལས་ཁུངས་མ་ལག་ཟུར་དུ་ཡོད་པའི་རྒྱལ་ཁབ་བཅུ་གྲངས་ལས་མེད་ཀྱང་། ད་ཆ་དེ་འདྲའི་གློག་འཛུགས་ཡོད་པའི་རྒྱལ་ཁབ་བཅུ་འགྱུར་གྱིས་གྲངས་འཕར་ཕྱིན་ཡོད་རེད། འདི་ནི་འཁོར་ཡུག་གི་གནས་དོན་ཐོག་གཞུང་ཐོག་ནས་དོ་སྣང་བྱེད་ཀྱི་ཡོད་པའི་རྟགས་པ་ཞིག་རེད། ལྷག་པར་འདས་མ་ཐག་པའི་ལོ་ངོ་བཅུ་ཕྲག་གཉིས་རིང་རྒྱལ་ཁབ་ཕལ་ཆེ་བས་འཁོར་ཡུག་སྲུང་སྐྱོབ་ཆེད་ཁྲིམས་ལུགས་ཡོད་བཞིན་ལ་བསྒྱུར་ཞིབ་དང་ ཟར་མེད་ཁྲིམས་ལུགས་གསར་གཏོད་བྱས་པ་སོགས་བྱུང་ཡོད་རེད། ལས་འགུལ་འདི་རིགས་མངའ་སྡེ་དང་ས་གནས་སོ་སོར་ཡང་སྤེལ་གཏོད་ལག་བསྟར་བྱེད་བཞིན་རེད།

རྒྱལ་སྤྱིའི་ཐད་ནས་བྱས་ནའང་། ད་ཆ་འཁོར་ཡུག་ཉེན་བཅད་སྲུང་སྐྱོབ་ཆེད་དང་རང་བྱུང་ཐོན་རྫས་རྣམས་ལ་རྒྱ་མཚན་ཟབ་པས་ཡོངས་སྤྱོད་བྱ་ནུས་བཅས་ཀྱི་ཆེད་རྒྱལ་སྤྱིའི་ཆིངས་ཡིག་གྲོས་མཐུན་ཁག་ ༤༠ ཙམ་ཡོད་རེད།

ཕྱི་ཁམས་འཁོར་ཡུག་ཐོག་ཤེས་ཡོན་སློབ་སྦྱོང་དང་དོན་གཉེར།

འཁོར་ཡུག་གི་གནས་དོན་སྐོར་གལ་ཆེར་ངོས་འཛིན་བྱས་ཏེ་སློབ་གྲྭ་དང་མཐོ་སློབ་ཁག་ཕལ་ཆེ་བར་འདི་སྐོར་སློབ་ཚན་དམིགས་བསལ་ཟུར་འཛུགས་བྱས་ཡོད། རྒྱལ་སྤྱིའི་ཉམས་ཞིབ་ཚིག་མཛོད་ཞིག་ལྟར་ན། ཉུང་མཐར་ཡང་སློབ་གཉེར་ཁང་ ༢༩༨ ནས་འཁོར་ཡུག་དང་འབྲེལ་ཡོད་སློབ་ཚན་སྣ་ཚོགས་ཐོག་དམིགས་བསལ་སློབ་སྦྱོང་

སྣོད་ཐོན་བྱེད་བཞིན་རེད་ཅེས་བཀོད་ཡོད།

གནས་ཚུལ་གསལ་བསྒྲགས་ཀྱི་ཐབས་ལམ་རྣམས་ལ་བརྟེན་ནས་འཁོར་ཡུག་གི་གནས་སྟངས་སྐོར་སྤྱི་ཡོངས་དོ་སྣང་དང་དོན་གཉེར་ཆེ་རུ་ཕྱིན་ཡོད། ཚགས་ཤོག་ཕལ་ཆེ་བའི་ནང་འཁོར་ཡུག་སྐོར་དམིགས་བསལ་རྩོམ་བྲིས་སྤེལ་འདོན་བྱེད་ཀྱི་ཡོད་རེད། འཁོར་ཡུག་གི་རྐྱེན་ངན་གནས་ཚུལ། དཔེར་ན། རྒྱ་གར་གྱི་བོ་པལ་གྲོང་ཁྱེར་དང་། རུ་སུའི་ཅར་ནོ་བལ། སུད་སིའི་གཙང་པོ་རེ་ཡིན་བཅས་ལ་བྱུང་བའི་རྐྱེན་ངན་གནས་ཚུལ་རྣམས་ཁྱབ་བསྒྲགས་ཤ་ཚང་ཆེན་པོ་ཕྱིན་ཡོད་རེད། འཁོར་ཡུག་ཐོག་དོན་གཉེར་ཆེ་རུ་ཕྱིན་པ་ལ་བརྟེན་ནས་མང་ཤ། །ཚོགས་ཁྲོད་དུ་སྲུང་སྐྱོབ་ཀྱི་ལས་འགུལ་ཆེ་ཕྲ་མང་པོ་གསར་གཏོད་ཡོད་བཞིན་རེད།

དམིགས་བསལ་ཐབས་བྱུས་ཁག

འཁོར་ཡུག་བཙོག་ཕྱད་ཀྱི་ཉེས་སྐྱོན་རྣམས་སེལ་འགོག་སླད་དམིགས་བསལ་འཕྲུལ་ལས་ཀྱི་ཐབས་བྱུས་ཤིན་ཏུ་མང་པོ་ཡོད། ལས་འགུལ་འདི་རིགས་ཐོག་མར་འཕྲུལ་ལས་ཡར་རྒྱས་ལྡན་པའི་རྒྱལ་ཁབ་ཁག་ཏུ་ལག་ལེན་བྱུང་སྟེ། ལས་འགུལ་དེ་དག་ཐོག་ད་ཆ་འགྲོ་གྲོན་ཡོ་རེ་ནས་འཕར་སྣོན་བྱེད་བཞིན་རེད།

དཔལ་འབྱོར་གྱི་ལས་ཐབས།

འཁོར་ཡུག་བདག་སྐྱོང་དང་ཉེས་སྐྱོན་རིགས་འགོག་སླད་དཔལ་འབྱོར་གྱི་ལས་ཐབས་མང་པོ་ཡང་ལག་བསྟར་བྱེད་བཞིན་རེད། ལས་ཐབས་འདི་དག་ནི། འཁོར་ཡུག་ལ་བཙོག་ཕྱད་སོགས་ཉེས་སྐྱོན་ཡོང་གཞིའི་ལས་ཁག་ལ་དམིགས་བསལ་ཁྲལ་འགེལ་བྱེད་པ་དང་། འཁོར་ཡུག་ཡར་རྒྱས་ལས་འགུལ་འབྲེལ་ཡོད་བཅས་ལ་དཔལ་འབྱོར་གྱི་ཆ་ཡངས་གཏོང་བ་སོགས་རེད།

༣ མ་འོངས་པར་དགོས་མཁོའི་གནས།

མི་འབོར་གྲངས་འཕེལ་འགྲོ་བ་དང་མཉམ་དུ་མི་ཚེའི་གནས་སྟངས་ཡར་རྒྱས་ལ་དོན་གཉེར་ཅན་གྱི་མི་གྲངས་ཀྱང་འཕེལ་ངེས་ཡིན་པ་དང་། དེ་ལ་བརྟེན་ནས་རང་བྱུང་ཐོན་ཟོག་ཁག་དང་འཁོར་ཡུག་འདོད་ཡོན་ལོངས་སྤྱོད་ལ་འང་ཕན་གནོད་དངོས་སུ་འབྲེལ་བ་ཞིག་རེད། དེར་བརྟེན་མ་འོངས་ཐོན་མཐོང་གི་ཐབས་བྱུས་གང་འདྲ་ཞིག་ལ་བརྟེན་ནས་སྐབས་སོ་སོའི་མིའི་འདོད་པ་ཁེངས་པ་དང་སྣོད་ཀྱི་འཁོར་ཡུག་ལ་ཚབས་ཆེའི་གནོད་སྐྱོན་མི་འབྱུང་ཞིག་བྱ་དགོས་པར་བསམ་ཞིབ་བྱ་རྒྱུ་གལ་ཆེན་པོ་རེད།

འདི་ཐད་དུ་ཆ་ཟུར་ཡོད་འཚོ་གནས་ཐུབ་ཐོག་ནས་ཡར་རྒྱས་ལས་འགུལ་བཅས་ཐུབ་ཡ་ཞིག་བྱུང་ན་ཁོང་གི་ཉེན་འགན་ལ་གཏོང་ཞེན་ཐུབ་པར་ངོས་འཛིན་བྱེད་ཀྱི་ཡོད་རེད། གཞི་རྩའི་དམིགས་ཡུལ་འདི་འགྲུབ་ཆེད་གཤམ་གསལ་ཐབས་ཚུལ་ཁག་ལ་ལག་ལེན་བསྟར་དགོས།

༧། ༌སྒྲིག་འཛུགས་ལྟ་ཚོགས།

འཁོར་ཡུག་སྲུང་སྐྱོབ་དང་ཡར་རྒྱས་ཆེད་དམིགས་བསལ་གཞུང་གི་སྒྲིག་འཛུགས་ཇི་ཡོད་རྣམས་ཡར་རྒྱས་ལྟ་ཚོགས་བྱ་རྒྱུ་གལ་ཆེན་པོ་རེད། དེ་དག་ལ་ཡར་རྒྱས་ལས་འགུལ་རིགས་རྩོམ་སྣད་འཆར་གཞི་འགོད་སྒྲིག་དང་འགྲོ་གྲོན་ཇི་དགོས་བཅས་ཀྱི་མཐུན་རྐྱེན་སྦྱར་རྒྱུ་དེ་བས་གལ་ཆེན་པོ་རེད།

འཁོར་ཡུག་ལ་བདག་སྐྱོང་རྩིས་བཤེར།

རྒྱལ་ཁབ་ཀྱི་དཔལ་འབྱོར་ནོར་ཡོན་ལ་བདག་སྲུང་དང་རྩིས་བཤེར་བྱེད་པ་བཞིན་དུ། འཁོར་ཡུག་གི་རྒྱ་ནང་ཞིང་ས་སོགས་ཀྱི་སྤུས་ཚད་དང་ལེགས་བཅོས་སོགས་ལ་ཡང་བདག་སྲུང་དང་རྩིས་བཤེར་བྱ་རྒྱུ་དང་། དེ་དག་གི་ཆེད་དུ་འགྲོ་གྲོན་སོགས་ཐབ་ཆ་ཟུར་འདོག་བྱུང་ན་དགེ་མཚན་ཆེན་པོ་ཡོང་གི་རེད།

སྲིལ་པའི་ངོས་སྦྱོངས།

འཁོར་ཡུག་སྲུང་སྐྱོབ་ཆེད་ཉེས་སྐྱོན་སྣང་འཛིན་པོ་ན་ཧ་བུ་མ་ཡིན་པར། ཉེས་སྐྱོན་འགོག་ཐབས་དང་། ཕྱག་པར་ཇོན་འགོག་བྱ་ཚུལ་སོགས་གནས་ཚུལ་ཡོངས་རྫོགས་ལ་སློབ་སྦྱོང་དང་ཟབ་པའི་གོ་ནས་ལས་འགུལ་རིགས་རྩོམ་དགོས་ཤིང་། དེ་འདྲ་འབྱུང་བར་ཐོག་མར་གནས་ཚུལ་དེ་དག་སྲིལ་ཚང་གི་ངོས་སྦྱོང་བྱ་རྒྱུ་གལ་ཆེར་ངོས་འཛིན་བྱེད་བཞིན་རེད།

ལག་ལེན་དང་ལྟ་བརྟན།

འཁོར་ཡུག་སྲུང་སྐྱོབ་དང་ཡར་རྒྱས་ཆེད་ཁྲིམས་ལུགས་ཇི་ཡོད་རྣམས་ལག་ལེན་དོན་འཁེལ་ཡོང་སླད་འཆར་གཞི་དང་དཔལ་འབྱོར་སོགས་གང་ས་ནས་མཐུན་རྐྱེན་སྦྱར་ཏེ་ལག་ལེན་ཞིབ་ཐབས་བྱ་དགོས། འདི་དག་ཐོག་དམིགས་བསལ་གྱི་ལྟ་བརྟན་རིགས་སྤྲོད་ཐུབ་ན་ཕན་ཐོགས་ཡོང་གི་རེད།

ཐབས་ཚུལ་ཁྱབ་བསྒྲགས།

འཁོར་ཡུག་གི་གང་ཅིའི་གནས་དོན་རྣམས་མང་ཚོགས་ལ་ཁྱབ་བསྒྲགས་ཐུབ་པ་གལ་ཆེན་རེད།

ཡ་རབས་བཟང་སྤྱོད་ཀྱི་ཡར་རྒྱས།

ལས་དོན་ཇི་འདྲ་ཞིག་ཡིན་རུང་གྲུབ་འབྲས་ལེགས་པོ་ཐོན་པར་མཐར་ཐུག་གི་རྐྱེན་རྩའི་ཐོག་ཏུ་བུགས་སྐྱིལ་དགོས་ཕལ་ཆེར་གྱིས་འདོད་ཀྱི་ཡོད་པ་ལྟར། འཁོར་ཡུག་གི་སྤུས་ཚད་དང་རང་བྱུང་ཐོན་རྫས་རྣམས་ཀྱི་ལོངས་སྤྱོད་བྱ་ཚུལ་བཅས་ཀྱང་མཐར་གཏུགས་ན། མི་བྱེ་བྲག་སོ་སོའི་གང་ཅིའི་སྤྱོད་ཚུལ་འཁྱེར་སྟངས་དང་ལག་ལེན་བཅས་ལ་རགས་ལུས་པ་ཞིག་རེད། མི་བྱེ་བྲག་མང་པོའི་སྤྱོད་ཚུལ་གཞན་ལ་དཔེ་སྟོན་ཐུབ་པའི་རིགས་བྱུང་ན། སྤྱི་ཡོངས་ལ་ཕན་གནོད་ཆེན་པོ་འབྲེལ་གྱི་རེད། དེར་བརྟེན་མི་ཞིར་རེ་རེ་ནས་ཀུན་སློང་དང་

སྤྱོད་ཚུལ་བཅོས་ཏེ་ཡར་རབས་བཟང་སྤྱོད་ལ་བསྐུལ་ཐུབ་ན་རང་ཤུགས་ཀྱིས་ཕན་ཐོགས་ཆེན་པོ་འབྱུང་ངེས་རེད། སློབ་ཚགས་གཞན་ལ་སྙིང་བརྩེ་དང་བཟོད་བསྲན་བྱེད་པ། སློབ་ཟླ་ཡོངས་ལ་བརྩེ་སྐྱོང་བྱེད་པ། རང་བྱུང་འཁོར་ཡུག་ལ་དབང་བསྒྱུར་བྱ་འདོད་ཀྱི་བསམ་བློ་དོར་ཏེ། དེ་དག་གི་ཁམས་གཉིས་དང་མཐུན་པར་སྤྱོད་པ། རང་བྱུང་ཐོན་རྫས་རྣམས་དང་འཁོར་ཡུག་གི་འདོད་ཡོན་རྣམས་ད་ལྟ་དང་མ་འོངས་པའི་མི་རབས་གཉིས་ཀའི་ཐུན་མོང་གི་མཁོ་ཕན་ཆེད་སྤྱོད་པ། དགོས་མེད་ཀྱི་སྤྱོད་ཐལ་མི་བྱེད་པ་བཅས་ནི་གཞི་རྩའི་སྤྱོད་ཚུལ་དང་ལག་ལེན་ཀྱང་འཕེལ་གཏོང་དགོས་རྣམས་རེད།

སྟོན་པ་ཤཱཀྱ་ཐུབ་པས་ལོ་ཉིས་སྟོང་བརྒལ་བའི་གོང་དུ་ཡ་རབས་ཀྱི་སྤྱོད་ཚུལ་འདི་དག་གཞན་ལ་བསྟན་པ་དང་རང་གིས་ཉམས་བཞེས་གནང་ཡོད་རེད། སྤྱོད་ཚུལ་འདི་དག་ནི་དེང་སང་ཡང་ཉམས་ལེན་བྱ་འོས་ཙམ་དུ་མ་ཟད། ལྷག་པར་ཡང་ཕན་འབྲེལ་ཆེན་པོར་གྱུར་ཡོད་རེད།

ད་ལྟ་དང་མ་འོངས་པར་དགོས་མཁོ་ཞེས་པའི་ཆོས་བྲིས་འདི་ནི། ཀྱི་ཙ་གཞིར་རེ་རེ་ནས་འཁོར་ཡུག་གི་གཞི་རྩའི་གནས་ཚུལ་གལ་ཆེ་རྣམས་ལ་དོན་གཉེར་དང་འབྲེལ། དེ་དང་འབྲེལ་བའི་ཡ་རབས་ཀྱི་སྤྱོད་ཚུལ་དང་ལག་ལེན་ཐུབ་པའི་ཆེད་དུ་བརྩམས་པ་ཡིན།། །།

·····བྱི་ཁམས་འཁོར་ཡུག་གི་གང་ཅིའི་གནས་ཚུལ་སྐོར་ལ་མཁས་དབང་ཉོག་ཞར་ཞེས་ཀྲུན་ནས་བརྩམས་པའི་གོང་གསལ་ཆོས་བྲིས་དབྱིན་སྐད་ཐོག་ནས་བརྗོད་དོན་སྙིང་བསྡུས་ཤིག་བོད་སྐད་དུ་ཕབ་བསྒྱུར་བྱས་པ་དང་། རྒྱས་ཞིབ་ཕབ་བསྒྱུར་ཡང་བྱེད་བཞིན་ཡིན་པ་བཅས།། །།

༄༅། ནང་ཆོས་ཐོག་ནས་རང་བྱུང་ཁམས་ལ་རྟ་ཕྱོགས་ཀྱི་ལས་འགུལ།

ནན་སི་ནེ་ཁེ།

༄༅། ནང་ཆོས་ཐོག་ནས་རང་བྱུང་ཁམས་ལ་རྟ་ཕྱོགས་ཀྱི་ལས་འགུལ་འདི་ནི་ནང་པ་ནང་ཁུལ་གྱི་རང་བྱུང་ཁམས་ཐོག་རྟ་ཚུལ་དང་། རྟ་སྲུང་ལེགས་སུ་གཏོང་རྒྱུའི་སློབ་གསོའི་ལས་འགུལ་ཞིག་ཡིན་ལ་འཛམ་གླིང་སི་མང་ཡོངས་ནས་ཡ་རབས་སྤྱོད་བཟང་གི་ཐོག་ནས་རང་བྱུང་། ཁམས་སྲུང་སྐྱོབ་བྱེད་རྒྱུར་དོ་སྣང་ཡོང་བའི་ཆེད་དུ་ཡང་ཡིན།

ཉེ་བའི་ལོ་བཅུ་ཕྲག་འགའ་ཤས་ནང་མིའི་ཤེས་བྱ་རིག་པ་དང་། ཚན་རིག་གི་གསར་གཏོད་གྲུབ་འབྲས་ནི་ཧ་ལས་དགོས་པ་ཞིག་བྱུང་ཡོད་པ་རེད། ཡིན་ནའང་ང་ཚོས་ངོ་མཚར་སྐྱེ་བའི་གྲུབ་འབྲས་དེ་དག་དང་མཉམ་པའམ། ཡང་ན་དེ་ལས་ཉུག་པའི་རང་བྱུང་ཁམས་ལ་གནོད་བསྐྱོད་པར་ཞིག་གི་ཉམས་ཆགས་ཆེན་པོ་བྱུང་ཡོད་པ་རེད། གནོད་བསྐྱེད་དེ་དག་ནི་དུས་ཚོད་ཐུང་ངུའི་ནང་གཞི་རྒྱ་ཆེན་པོ་ཞིག་བཏང་བའི་རྐྱེན་གྱིས་སོ་ནམ་དང་འབྲོང་བརྙན་སོགས་ལ་དམིགས་བསལ་གྱི་དོ་སྣང་བྱེད་རྒྱུར་འགོག་རྐྱེན་མང་པོ་ཞིག་བཟོས་ཡོད་པ་རེད།

རང་བྱུང་ཁམས་སྲུང་སྐྱོབ་བྱེད་རྒྱུ་དེ་ནི་གཞུང་དང་། སེར་གྱི་ཚོགས་པ་ཁག་གི་ཐོ་འཁྲིད་པའི་ལས་འགུལ་ཞིག་ཡིན་པ་དང་། དེ་ནི་འགྱོ་བ་མིའི་ལོ་རྒྱུས་ནང་ཉེ་བའི་ཆར་བྱུང་བའི་འགྱུར་བ་གསར་པ་ཞིག་ཀྱང་རེད། ལོ་བཅུ་ཕྲག་འགའ་ཞིག་ཕྱིན་པའི་ལས་འགུལ་འདི་ནི་རྒྱལ་སྤྱིའི་ནང་གནད་འགག་ཆེ་བའི་ལས་འགུལ་ཞིག་ཡིན་ལ་ད་དུང་ངོས་འཛིན་དང་ཁྱབ་བདལ་རྒྱ་ཆེར་འགྲོ་ཐུབ་རེད།

སྤྱིར་འཛམ་གླིང་འདིའི་རྫོད་བཅུད་ཉམས་ཆགས་མི་འགྲོ་བའི་ཐབས་ལམ་དམིགས་བསལ་ཁ་གསལ་བ་ཞིག་མེད་ནའང་ང་ཚོས་རྟོགས་པའི་འཛམ་གླིང་འདི་བཞིན་དུ་ཨུར་རྒྱུན་རིང་གནས་ཐུབ་པའི་ཐབས་ཤེས་ཀྱི་སློབ་སྦྱོང་མང་པོ་ཞིག་བྱེད་རྒྱུ་དེ་ནི་གལ་ཆེ་ཤོས་ཤིག་ཆགས་ཡོད་པ་རེད། ད་ཡོད་རང་བྱུང་ཁམས་དང་། རང་བྱུང་གནས་ཀྱི་སྲུང་སྐྱོབ་བྱེད་རྒྱུའི་སློབ་གསོ་མང་ཆེ་བ་ནི་ང་ཚོར་བྲལ་སེལ་དཀའ་ངལ་འབྱུང་པའི་སྐབས་ཀྱི་ཐབས་ལམ་ཤ་སྟག་རེད། ད་ཆ་ཚན་རིག་གི་ཐོག་ནས་ཐོན་སྐྱེད་དང་། ཕྲུལ་ཆགས་ཀྱི་དཀའ་ངལ། བཟོ་བསྐྲུན་གྱི་དཀའ་ངལ་སོགས་དེ་དག་རྒྱུན་འཁྱོངས་ནས་སེལ་ཐབས་སུ་ཤུགས་རྫོན་ཤུགས་གི་ཡོད་པ་རེད།

རང་བྱུང་ཁོར་ཡུག་གི་སྲུང་སྐྱོབ་ལ་ཚན་རིག་གི་ལས་ཀ་ནི་མེད་དུ་མི་རུང་བ་ཞིག་རེད། ཚན་རིག་ཐོག་ནས་བརྟག་དཔྱད་ཞིབ་འཇུག་བྱས་རྗེས་གལ་གནད་ཆེ་ཆུང་དབྱེ་འབྱེད་ཀྱིས་འཛམ་གླིང་གི་འགོ་འཁྲིད་དང་། འཆར་གཞི་ཐག་གཅོད་བྱེད་མཁན་རྣམས་ལ་འབོད་བསྐུལ་གྱིས་རང་བྱུང་ཁམས་ལ་སྲུང་

སྐྱབ་ཐུབ་པ་དགོས་རྒྱུ། དཔེར་ན་མིའི་མ་རིག་པ་དང་། འདོད་ཆགས། ཁོར་ཡུག་ལ་བཅོ་ལེན་མེད་པའི་མི་ཡི་བྱ་སྤྱོད་ཀྱི་རྐྱེན་གྱིས་ལ་རྒྱུས་བརྒྱབ་པ་དང་། ཆུ་རློགས་མ་ཆགས་པ་སོགས་ཀྱི་དཀའ་ངལ་བྱུང་བ་ཞིག་རེད།

ནང་ཆོས་ནས་རང་བྱུང་ཁམས་ལ་ཧ་ཤུགས་ཀྱི་ལས་འགུལ་དེའི་ནང་ཚན་རིག་གཙོ་བོར་འཛིན་རྒྱུ་ཡིན། དེང་འཛམ་གླིང་ནང་མི་འབོར་ཇེ་ཆེར་འཕེལ་རྒྱས་འགྲོ་བཞིན་པ་དང་། མིའི་རེ་འདུན། དགོས་མཁོ་ཇེ་མང་དུ་ཕྱིན་པའི་སྐབས་དེར་འཛམ་གླིང་སྤྱོད་ཀྱི་བཟོ་མི་ཐུབ་པའི་ཁུངས་རྒྱུ་རྣམས་ཆེས་ཉུང་དུ་ཕྱིན་ཡོད་པ་རེད།

ལས་འགུལ་འདི་བཞིན་ཤེས་ཡོན་གྱི་ཐོག་ནས་ཧ་ཤུགས་གསར་པ་ཞིག་ཡིན་པ་མ་ཟད། འདིའི་ནང་འགྲོ་བ་མིའི་རིག་གཞུང་དང་། སྤྱི་ཚོགས་ཀྱི་གནས་སྟངས། འདུ་ཤེས་འཛིན་སྟངས། འདུ་ཤེས་འཛིན་སྟངས་སོགས་ལ་འཆང་གལ་ཆེར་བཅིས་ཏེ་ཙ་འཛིན་བྱེད་ཀྱི་ཡོད་པ་རེད། དེ་ཙ་དཀའ་ངལ་སེལ་ཐུབ་པའི་གལ་ཆེའི་ནུས་པ་ཡོད་པའི་ཤེས་ཡོན་གྱི་བསླབ་བྱ་དེ་ཚོར་དེ་ཙམ་གྱི་ངོ་རྒྱང་མ་བྲིད་པར་རྒྱང་ཆུང་བྱས་ཡོད་པ་རེད།

ནང་ཆོས་ཐོག་ནས་རང་བྱུང་ཁམས་ལ་ཧ་ཤུགས་ཀྱི་ལས་འགུལ་འདི་རི་ནང་ཐོག་མར་ཁྱིམ་ཚང་ཞིག་ནས་འགོ་ཚུགས་ཀྱི་དངོས་གཞིའི་སློབ་གསོ་དང་། འགོ་འཁྲིད་ཀྱི་འགན་དབང་བར་ཤེས་ཡོན་གྱི་ངོ་པོ་ཆ་ཚང་བ་ཞིག་ཡོད། ཁྱིམ་ཚང་རེ་རེ་དང་། གྲོང་རྡེ་སོ་སོའི་ནང་ཐུན་མོང་མ་ཡིན་པའི་ཁྱད་ཆོས་རིག་གཞུང་དང་། ཡ་རབས་ཀུན་སྤྱོད་ཀྱི་ཐོག་ནས་ཤེས་ཡོན་ཕེལ་ཐུབ་ཀྱི་ཡོད་པ་རེད། ཤེས་ཡོན་དེའི་ནང་སོ་ ༣༥༠༠ ཉག་ཙམ་རྗེན་གྱི་ནང་བའི་ཕྱུག་དཔེ་དང་། རྗེས་རིས་སོགས་ནས་རང་བྱུང་ཁམས་སྲུང་སྐྱོབ་དགོས་པའི་སློབ་གསོ་རྣམས་བརྗོ་རྒྱབ་ཀྱི་དེབ་ཆུང་དང་། གློག་བརྙན་སོགས་ནས་དེང་དུས་ཤེས་ཡོན་སྤྲོད་ལྡངས་ཀྱི་ལམ་ནས་སྤྱི་ཚོགས་ནང་སློབ་གསོ་སྤྲོད་ཐུབ་ཀྱི་ཡོད་པ་རེད།

ཕྱི་ལོ་ ༡༩༨༥ ལོར་འགོ་བཙུགས་པའི་ཉམས་ཞིབ་ལས་འགུལ་འདི་ནི་བོད་གཞུང་ཆོས་རིག་ལྷན་ཁང་དང་། བོད་གཞུང་དྲིལ་བསྒྲགས་ལྷན་ཁང་གཉིས་ནས་ཐེག་པ་ཆེན་པོའི་གཞུང་ནས་ཉམས་ཞིབ་གནང་རྒྱུ་དང་། ཐཱ་ཡི་ལེན་ཊོ་རི་དྲགས་ཚོགས་པ་དང་། ཐཱ་ཡི་གཞུང་གི་ཤེས་རིག་ལྷན་ཁང་། ཐ་མ་ས་མཐོ་སློབ་བཅས་ནས་ཐེག་དམན་གྱི་གཞུང་ལུགས་ནས་ཉམས་ཞིབ་ཀྱིས་འགོ་ཚུགས་བྱེད་རྒྱུ་ཡིན། ཐོག་མར་བོད་དང་ཐཱ་ཡི་ལེན་ཊོའི་ནང་པ་ནས་འགོ་བཙུགས་པའི་ལས་འགུལ་ཞིག་ཡིན་ནའང་ལས་དོན་ཉམས་ཞིབ་བྱས་པའི་སྐབས་ནང་པའི་རྒྱལ་ཁབ་གཞན་དང་། སྤྱི་ཚོགས་ཁག་ལ་འབྲེལ་བ་རྒྱ་ཆེ་བྱུང་ཡོད།པ་དེ་ནི་དགའ་བསུའི་རང་བཞིན་ཡིན་པ་དང་། ལས་འགུལ་འདི་ནི་ནང་པའི་གཞུང་དང་། ཚོགས་པ། གིར་པ་ལུ་རུང་གི་བེད་སྤྱོད་བྱེད་འདོད་ཡོད་པ་རྣམས་ལ་སློབ་གསོའི་ཡིག་ཆ་དང་། དཔར་

དཔེ་སོགས་སྤྲོད་རྒྱུའི་དམིགས་ཡུལ་ཡོད་པ་རེད།

ཤེས་ཡོན་སློབ་སྦྱོང་སྤྲོད་སྟངས་གསར་པའི་འདིར་ནང་པའི་ཆོས་དེ་བཞིན་ངོ་ཚོད་ཀྱི་ཆེད་དུ་འདེམས་སྒྲུག་བྱས་པ་ཞིག་ཡིན། ནང་ཆོས་གཞུང་ལུགས་ཀྱི་བསླབ་བྱ་རྣམས་ཡུན་རིང་རྒྱུན་བརྟན་གནས་པའི་རིག་པའི་གཞུང་ཞིག་ཡིན་པ་དང་། སེམས་ཅན་ཐམས་ཅད་ཡིད་ལ་དྲན་ཏེ་བྱམས་སྙིང་རྗེ་བྱེད་དགོས་པའི་བསླབ་བྱ་ཡོད་པ་རེད། དེ་བཞིན་ཨེ་ཤི་ཡའི་གླིང་ཆེན་ས་ཁུལ་མང་པོའི་ནང་ཐུན་མོང་མ་ཡིན་པའི་རི་དྭགས་རིགས་མང་པོ་ཞིག་ཅ་ཅོ་ངས་འགྱོ་ཉེན་ཡོད་པར་བརྟེན་ནང་པའི་བསླབ་བྱ་དེ་དག་ཕན་ནུས་ཆེ་ལ་གཞི་རྒྱ་ཆེ་བར་ཐེབ་ཐུབ་ཀྱི་ཡོད་པ་རེད། དེ་བཞིན་ཨེ་ཤི་ཡའི་ཤར་གསེབ་ས་ཁུལ་མང་པོའི་ནང་སློབ་སྦྱོང་བྱེད་རྒྱུར་ནང་པའི་ཆོས་ཀྱི་བསླབ་བྱ་དེ་གཙོ་བོ་ཡིན་སྟབས་ནང་པའི་ཆོས་ཀྱི་ཐོག་ནས་ཅ་ཅོ་ངས་འགྱོ་ཉེན་གྱི་སྲོག་ཆགས་ཀྱི་རིགས་དེ་དག་སྲུང་སྐྱོབ་བྱ་རྒྱུར་ཕན་ནུས་ཤུགས་ཆེ་ཡོད་པ་རེད།

འཛམ་གླིང་རྒྱལ་ཁབ་གང་སར་རང་བྱུང་ཁམས་སྲུང་སྐྱོབ་བྱེད་རྒྱུར་དོ་སྣང་ཤུགས་ཆེ་ཡོད་པར་བརྟེན་ནང་ཆོས་ཐོག་ནས་ལས་འགུལ་ཐེལ་བཀོད་དང་། ཆོས་ལུགས་གཞན་ཁག་རྣམས་དང་འབྲེལ་གཏུག་གིས་འཆར་གཞི་གསར་བཟོ་ཐུབ་རྒྱུར་ཡང་ཕན་ཐོགས་ཆེན་པོ་ཡོད་པ་ཞིག་རེད།

ནང་ཆོས་ཐོག་ནས་རང་བྱུང་ཁམས་ལ་ངོ་རྟོགས་ཀྱི་ལས་འགུལ་འདི་བཞིན་རྒྱལ་སྤྱིའི་གལ་གནད་ཆེ་བའི་ཚོགས་པ་ཁག་དང་། གེར་པ་མང་པོས་རྒྱབ་སྐྱོར་གནང་བ་རྣམས་ལ་ང་ཚོས་སྙིང་ཐག་པ་ནས་ཐུགས་རྗེ་ཆེ་ཞུ་རྒྱུ་དང་། དགའ་བསུའི་ངང་གཏམ་དུ་མཚོན་གཞུང་བཀོད་རྒྱུ་ཡིན།

རྒྱལ་སྐུ་ནན་སི་ཋེ་ཕི་མཆོག་ནང་ཆོས་ཐོག་ནས་རང་བྱུང་ཁམས་ལ་ངོ་རྟོགས་ཀྱི་ལས་འགུལ་འབུ་འཛུགས་མཁན་དང་། དེའི་སྐོར་རྒྱལ་སྤྱིའི་ནང་འགོ་འཁྲིད་མཁན་ཡིན། ཁོང་ནས་ད་བར་སྲོག་ཆགས་དང་རང་བྱུང་ཁམས་སྲུང་སྐྱོབ་སྐོར་རྩོམ་བྲིས་ཁག ༡༠ སྐྲུག་གནང་ཡོད། རྒྱ་ནག་རྒྱལ་སྤྱིའི་རི་དྭགས་ཚོགས་པ་གསར་འཛུགས་ཀྱི་འབྲེལ་ལམ་འཆར་འདོན་ཡང་ཁོང་ནས་གནང་ཡོད་པ་རེད།།